Second Person Queer

# Second Person Queer

## Who you are (so far)

edited by Richard Labonté and Lawrence Schimel

ARSENAL PULP PRESS

VANCOUVER

ARSENAL PULP PRESS
Suite 200, 341 Water Street
Vancouver, BC
Canada  V6B 1B8
*arsenalpulp.com*

The publisher gratefully acknowledges the support of the Canada Council for the Arts and the British Columbia Arts Council for its publishing program, and the Government of Canada through the Book Publishing Industry Development Program and the Government of British Columbia through the Book Publishing Tax Credit Program for its publishing activities.

Text and cover design by Shyla Seller
Cover photograph © JupiterImages, *comstock.com*

"An Apology to My Mother" © 2006 by S. Bear Bergman. First published in *Butch Is a Noun*, Suspect Thoughts Press, 2006, and reprinted with the author's permission.

A selection from *Funeral Rites* by Jean Genet appears in "Every Room After" by Jason Timermanis. Copyright © 1969 by Grove Press, Inc. Used by permission of Grove/Atlantic, Inc.

Printed and bound in Canada

**Library and Archives Canada Cataloguing in Publication**


Second person queer : who you are (so far) / edited by Richard Labonté and Lawrence Schimel.


ISBN 978-1-55152-245-6


1. Homosexuality.  2. Bisexuality.  3. Transsexualism.
I. Labonté, Richard, 1949-  II. Schimel, Lawrence

HQ75.15.S42 2009        306.76'6        C2008-908138-2

# Contents

Introduction  7   Richard Labonté and Lawrence Schimel

*Looking into the Queer View Mirror*
You Know You Know  *13*   Blair Mastbaum
How Not to Be Offended by Everything: A Guide for Asian Men
      *16*   Viet Dinh
You Are Here  *19*   Stacey May Fowles
You Bear, Me Jane  *23*   R.M. Vaughan
How to Label Yourself, or Not  *27*   B.J. Epstein
Every Room After: Notes to Jean Genet  *30*   Jason Timermanis
To My Sisters and Brothers in Hiding  *34*   Roz Kaveney
How to Hate Yourself Completely  *41*   Natty Soltesz


*Getting Your Queer On*
Why You *Should* Have Sex on the First Date  *47*   Steven Bereznai
How to Date a Married Man  *55*   Lewis DeSimone
How to Conjure Dead Poets  *60*   Julie R. Enszer
How to Be a Happy Slut (Five Easy Steps to Gay Whoredom)  *64*
      Sky Gilbert
How to Divine Your Fetish  *68*   Suki Lee
How to Love Your Inner Femme ( … Because We All Have One)
      *73*   Mette Bach


*Queer Wisdom: Our Past, Present, and Future*
An Apology to My Mother  *79*   S. Bear Bergman
An Open Letter to the Newly Bisexual Gay Kid  *82*   Daniel Allen
      Cox
Some Notes to a Young Not-Yet-Femme  *86*   Maggie Crowley
Insider Info for a Foster Nephew  *90*   Wes Hartley
To My Thirteen-Year-Old Daughter, Who Just Told Me She's Bi
      *95*   Sean Michael Law

Letter to a New Generation of Gate Keepers  99  Lloyd Meeker
Advice for My Younger Self  104  Andy Quan
Letter to a Young Man in Early Winter from a Train, or How to
    Love  108  Michael Rowe

*Practically Queer*
Hopes, Dreams, and a Little Marriage Advice  117  Dr Kevin
    Alderson
How to Archive Our History  123  Jane Van Ingen
How to Write and Live to Tell about It  127  Victor J. Banis
How to Survive Gay Celebrity: A Pocket Guide  131  Paul Bellini
The Do's and Don'ts of Getting Married for a Green Card  137
    Tony Correia
How to Bury Our Dead  141  Amber Dawn
How to Throw a Women's Playparty  150  Elaine Miller
Ten Principles for the Good Gay Man  159  Jay Starre
Fifty Suggestions for the Aftermath  163  Achy Obejas
How Not to Fall for a Lesbian Celebrity  167  Joy Parks

*Finding Yourself, Queerly*
How to Choose a Cock  173  Terry Goldie
Someday Your Prince May Come ... Not That You'll Listen to Me
    176  Greg Herren
Family Family (This One's for the Kids)  180  Arden Eli Hill
Leather Queer: Learning the Ropes  185  Alisa Lemberg
How to Be a Country Leather Bear  188  Jeff Mann
How to Be a Visible Femme  194  Stacia Seaman
Bottoms Up  198  Clarence Wong
Just This Moment: A Letter to David Wojnarowicz  203  Mattilda
    Bernstein Sycamore

Contributors' biographies  209
Editors' biographies  222

# INTRODUCTION

## How to Read This Book

So. Who are you, so far?

The answer, we hope, is that you are part of everyone in this book—and that everyone in this book is part of you. *Second Person Queer* is not a book of rules, not a manual of mandatory instructions on how to be a good queer, not a definitive guide on how to live a (L)esbian or (G)ay or (B)isexual or (T)ransgender or (Q)uestioning (or Queer) life. It's not just a collection of coming-out essays (though it can be read as an eclectic how-to compendium).

Enough of the nots. Here is what this book is: like its predecessor, *First Person Queer*, *SPQ* is a snapshot of contemporary queer life. But its forty contributors—both seasoned homosexuals speaking from years of experience, and new-minted dykes and fresh-faced fags excited about who they're in the process of becoming—also reach back into their experiential pasts or peer into their possible futures to inform you about essential queer facts or to inspire you in your journey toward identity and understanding.

*SPQ* is a mirror of who you are, or perhaps of the person you would most like to be. Read it if you're just coming out; read it if you came out long ago but are curious about another letter from the LGBTQ alphabet; read what queer elders and youngsters have to say, sometimes seriously and sometimes comically—but always wisely and always in the spirit of sharing—about who you, and we, are.

That said, our contributors don't always agree with each other. Individual pieces suggest a particular physical, emotional, or spiritual stance, or outright exhort you to embrace or avoid a certain type of behavior; some promote opposing points of view—just like the LGBTQ(Q) community, which can be fractious, contentious, argumentative … you get the gist. *SPQ* collects a plurality of voices about a range of queer-interest topics, not always on the same page, but always with the same intention: to help you define (or, perhaps, decide) who you are.

And just as you'll make up your own rules for how to live your life, there are no hard and fast rules for how (or why) to read this book—despite the title of this introduction.

We've explained what we (as editors and as contributors) set out to do with this anthology, and now it's up to you to choose what you want to do with it. Some suggestions:

First, don't feel limited by the fact that we have organized this book thematically: skip your way through the collection, starting with a piece by a favorite author or a title that catches your eye— or perhaps with a subject that you are grappling with in your own life.

Discover yourself in this book: You're not so keen on gay pride, you're an Asian queer, you're a big bear, you have qualms about your trans peers, you find yourself reflected in literature, you question why you're here, you question labels, you have absorbed so much gay shame.

Learn from this book: You should have sex on a first date. You ought to date a married man. You have much to learn from your gay forebears. You can be a slut, and happy. You can be a top—or a bottom—and here's how to decide. You need to honor your inner femme—and here's how to reach her.

Glean advice from this book: From a daughter to her mother, from a queer man to a bisexual boy, from a queer woman to a femme girl, from a gay elder to all gay youth, from a gay father to his bisexual thirteen-year-old daughter, from a Two Spirit queer to his spiritual heirs, from a gay man to his younger self, from a man who loves him to a young friend.

Acquire practical knowledge from this book: What should you consider before getting married? How can you preserve your past? What are the tricks of the writing trade? How could you survive being a gay celebrity, should such a thing ever come to pass? Why should you avoid falling in love with a lesbian celebrity? What are the pitfalls of a marriage arranged for immigration reasons? How do you handle death? What are the organizational tools for pulling off a great queer event? And, by the numbers: consider ten principles a good gay man might live by, and count fifty ways to leave a lover.

Find your queer core in this book: Choose the perfect cock, find true love, build a trans family, become a leather queer, be a defiant country bear, embrace your femme self, age into your queer sexy self with dignity, learn the grace of queer activism.

In short: find information and inspiration and entertainment in these essays, find reassurance as you embark on, or continue in, your journey toward queer identity and understanding. Find yourself.

*Richard Labonté, Bowen Island, Canada*
*Lawrence Schimel, Madrid, Spain*

Looking into the Queer View Mirror

# You Know You Know

## Blair Mastbaum

Dear Gay Pride people:

You know they're watching. You know some of them are cringing. You know there's no reason to really be "proud" of a genetic condition. You know there's still inequality, but dancing on a float isn't any way to achieve your goals. You know the way to really make change is by making the change you want to see in others in yourself. You know it's fun for a lot of you. You know to some of us it just looks like you're showing off your many hours in the gym. You know that some of us think you guys are trying too hard. You know that some of you like to act like women, but you don't know why. You know that people who don't like you will seize footage of you to show their right-wing followers that you are ridiculous. You ride on floats, shirtless, waving to people, like you should be admired just for being yourself.

You know you shouldn't take crystal meth and obsess about sex and orgies and younger guys or older guys or Asian guys or Jewish guys or ginger-headed guys, but you do. You're making up for lost time, you say. You didn't get to slut around in high school, so you're doing it now at age thirty-three or forty-four or fifty-five. You act like you're proud, but really you're just as ashamed and self-conscious and scared and hopeful and happy and angsty and thrilled to be alive as anyone else. You think you're funnier than everyone else. You drive in convertibles and attend parties in shirts that cost too much. You join parties of people who look exactly like you do. You go to bear weekends on rivers. You find sex on Craigslist. You leave your small towns, most of you. You fit in easily sometimes in your new big cities. You wear baseball caps. You become dads. You read the newspaper or *Out* magazine. You get jobs at investment firms or you wait tables. You sell drugs. You sell out. You call yourself Log Cabin. You know you don't trust your dad. You form families out of people who aren't related to you. You say you like Mormon boys. You introduce your boyfriend as your lover or your partner or your husband. You go to Canada and get married and then get married again in San Francisco. You make more money than most people. You do more drugs. You smoke more cigarettes. You buy more Subarus. You do more speed. You hang out together at happy hour and throw your head back and laugh. You know the girls that have crushes on you. You radicalize and preach.

You move back to your small town and quit doing drugs and move in with your boyfriend and buy two cars. You start a restaurant. You drink too much behind the bar of your own restaurant. You go to AA even though you don't believe in God. You cringe even capitalizing the word God when you're writing it. You have a Facebook and a Manhunt and a MySpace page. You cancel your MySpace. You started your Real Jock account but forgot the password, and anyway, you're not a real jock. You hate Perez Hilton and Paris Hilton, but you like her little brother. You have huge parties. You want to get married. You think gay marriage is stupid. You slept with an underage kid. You painted your living room dark red. You have a bathroom painted black. You do lots of cocaine. You drink only vodka tonics because they're not fattening. You think about what you're eating. You know, you have to know, that every "gay" restaurant on earth has horrible food. You know, sometimes you think if you have to hear the word "gay" ever again, you might take a rusty knife and shove it into your heart. You know that David Sedaris is funny, but in a very sedate way. You know you have more pills in your medicine cabinet than your grandfather does. You know it's not okay, for the most part, to be gay in the African-American community, but you don't really do anything about it. You know it's basically the same for Latinos. You know that there are exceptions to every rule. You know most lesbians think you're ridiculous. You know you have a dog or a cat. You know you should go to the gym more. You know you should really stop eating pasta so much. You know you should volunteer to read to some inner city kids. You know you should give more of your money away, and not to the Human Rights Campaign, because they have such a horrendous track record.

You know you shouldn't have another cup of coffee. You know you shouldn't start looking at porn. You know where that will lead. You know, you should finally just admit that desiring another man (or woman if you're a woman) isn't anything to be proud of, and neither is categorizing yourself for everyone else. You know it only limits what you can become. You know that nothing much changes. You know you want new blinds in your dining room. You know you should move. You know you should call your mother—and your father. You know you shouldn't place your sexuality above everything else. You know that the people who do that aren't buying this book, most likely. You know all that matters is that you're happy. You know that sex is fun but not required—anytime, ever.

You know I'm not like you because I'm writing this. You think I'm lying or angry or weird. You think I'm being contrary, like you think when I say I like rainy days best and hate Los Angeles and ketchup. You know I wasted your time. You know, you must, that I can't believe I'm still writing about these things. You don't know why I can't just roll over and enjoy it. You're just like everyone else, so get over it.

You know if riding on a float makes you happy, it's worth it, but you don't have to.

# How Not To Be Offended by Everything: A Guide for Asian Men

## Viet Dinh

First of all, it's not small.

Of the daily insults you endure, this stings the most. Somehow, you ended up on the losing end of the racial/sexual stereotypes. Black men: athletic, virile, and well-proportioned. Latin men: fiery, feisty, and passionate. Asian men: feminine, submissive, and—well, you know.

Perhaps you conform to some of these: you *are* feminine; you *are* a bottom; you *are* fresh off the boat and *no speakee Engrish*. But stereotypes shouldn't define the entirety of who you are. Emphasize the traits that make you particular: your expertise in weaving baskets out of bamboo, your flair for spicing up instant Ramen noodles, your unerring eye for gold and jade jewelry. After all, you can't be held responsible for the ignorance of others.

Nonetheless, this will happen at least once. You go up to a guy, and he stops you in your tracks: "Sorry. I'm just not into Asians." If you're lucky, it'll only happen once, but be prepared to hear it again and again. You replay the incident in your head until every polite "not interested" or "thanks, but ..." becomes an echo of *I'm not into Asians*. Maybe you get angry on behalf of your entire race: who writes off a full half of the world's population? Or maybe you take solace in the meditation techniques of your ancestors: Zen, tai chi, *fuk yu suk mai kok*. But it cuts you in ways you can't imagine, and you find yourself staring at someone, wondering, *Will he like Asians?* before you wonder, *Will he like me?*

Certainly, you can find men who are particularly attracted to Asians—rice queens, they call themselves. You may be suspicious of their motives. Some of the men are older and heavyset; are Asians their race of last resort? Others wear boyfriends on their arms like colorful bangles; they talk about your exotic skin, your body, your lips, and you wonder if you are merely a blank screen upon which they can cast their colonialist projections. Remember, you don't have to follow any cultural sexual script. Don't limit yourself to being a houseboy, blushing geisha, rickshaw runner, servant boy, China doll, or male mail-order bride. You can also be a computer programmer, laundromat owner, railroad worker, Yakuza or Triad member, grocery shopkeeper, or—best of all—kung fu master.

Still, it's nice to be desired without having to face possible humiliation, even if Edward Said rolls in his grave when he sees you together. But don't let rice queens become a crutch. Plenty of men—of all races—aren't prejudiced towards your heritage or what you may or may not be packing in your pants. They may simply want a ride in your customized, nitrous-injected Honda—because if *The Fast and the Furious* has taught you anything, it's that hot men love pimped-out cars.

Potential paramours will ask, "What does your name mean?" Take this as an opportunity to exercise poetic license. Tell him that your name means "Light Morning Mist Rising Off of the Mountain Lake Shenzhou" or "Most Revered Heavenly Brother of the Fifth Celestial Palace." And if he looks at you with disbelief, explain that Asian languages, much like their cars and their workforce, are very efficient.

Maybe he's more cultured. He may have traveled to your country of origin or studied it or lived there. But remember, in the end, that he's a *gweilo*, and don't be afraid to remind him of the fact: "Didn't my grandfather go to war to keep you out of our business?"

But you also need to examine the origins of your own preferences. You know instinctively that desire makes its own demands, that everyone has his peculiar taste, but still—! If you're attracted primarily to white men, you'll hear plenty of explanations for this. Internalized racism. Cultural imperialism. Yearning for the unattainable. You might blame the media: After years of flipping through magazines and pornography chock full of beautiful white men with chiseled white features, you begin to forget what your own face looks like.

Whatever the case, you have to overcome your own jealousies. You're not in a contest to see who can get the richest, whitest, or most handsome boyfriend. When you see another gay Asian and white male couple, think, *Good for them!* instead of, *That thieving, whoring bitch!* You may have grown up in an ultra-competitive environment, with your parents pushing you to become a doctor or lawyer or electrical engineer. But don't perpetuate this streak; you can leave behind this influence the way you've left behind your mother's nagging voice, asking, "Why you no marry nice [ethnicity-appropriate] girl?"

Stand in front of a mirror. Sometimes, you'll wonder if there's any way to escape your own skin, and the answer is always *no*. Sometimes, you'll blame your parents—all those years of piano and violin lessons, and the boys haven't come beating down your door? And sometimes you'll see an okay, flawed human being who knows he needs some work but isn't afraid of thinking things through, even if they don't lead to any definitive answers. You can hold yourself for a moment and realize that it's not small at all. The real problem is that the more you think it's small, the smaller it gets.

Okay, maybe it *is* small. So what? There are worse things. You could be cruel, insensitive, or narcissistic. You could be critical of the faults of others and blind to your own. You could be so consumed with rage that it burns everyone with whom you come into contact. Or you could dust yourself off—there are worse injustices in the world—and continue. Find yourself someone who accepts you, faults and all, just as you accept all his faults. Hold him close and discover the different ways in which you grow.

# You Are Here

Stacey May Fowles

"You are here."

Or that's what the sign says. That's where the arrow points. That's what's been spelled out for you.

It's kind of the way life works. You wake up one day and all of a sudden—*you are here.*

Question is, *how did you get here?* Fact is, people are going to want to know the answer to this question. For some reason, people always need reasons—signposts, pigeonholes, and labels—need you to define where you are and why you're there and what that means. I'm pretty sure people need that because uncertainty scares them. People will need you to define and explain and excuse because chaos—the unknown—terrifies them.

Looks like you're going to have to make up an answer. The kind of people who need answers will prefer answers such as, "My dad left when I was ten" or, "My mother didn't hug me enough." They will accept excuses like, "It was university, and I was only experimenting." Stock answers that gloss over identity and ideology—they can file those conveniently and comfortably. They really like things to be easier for them, and not for you.

Why are you here?

Are you here because your mom was the type who burned her bra, smoked weed, and told you, "You can be and do anything you want"? Are you here because she didn't want you to "play house"— she thought it was a patriarchal construct to train young women to be subservient? Your mom seems pretty cool, actually.

But you played house anyway, didn't you? Sometimes you were

the husband and sometimes you were the wife. And then you played doctor, with that pretty, pigtailed blonde girl named Chrissie who lived two houses over. That girl taught you to kiss boys and then asked if you wanted to "compare parts" (and you, of course, obliged without contest). That girl taught you that secrets could be liberating and that something that felt wrong could be the best thing of all.

Maybe you're here because you've always been the type to question things. You were the kid in elementary school whose hand predictably shot up at the back of the class, your question always, "But why?" Every time they separated the boys from the girls, you questioned. Every time you were told what to wear, what to read, what to listen to, you questioned. Every time they said, "Girls are supposed to …" you kicked up a little-girl-temper-tantrum fuss. "No, no, no, no," you wailed.

People made you feel it was wrong to query, to ask why, but you kept doing it anyway, that itch too fierce not to be scratched. It wasn't enough to hear "Because I said so." And it still isn't.

So when it was time to like boys, you questioned that as well. It wasn't that you knew you didn't like them, you just wondered why it was implied that you would be dressing and painting yourself to please them, fawning all over them breathlessly while writing your first name attached to their last names in purple cursive handwriting.

Maybe you're here because you didn't want to kiss Tommy in the back of his mom's beige Buick LeSabre after he took you to see *Titanic* and bought you a quarter-chicken dinner at Swiss Chalet. No offence to Tommy, but for some reason you couldn't quite figure out, he just *wasn't your type*.

When you broke up with him one day after school, he called you a "fucking frigid dyke."

Are you here because you didn't want to go to the prom? Or maybe you really wanted to go, really wanted to wear a pink chiffon dress and a yellow rose tied to your wrist, but your best friend Suzy didn't want to go with you? "We could go as friends. It'll be so much more fun than this boyfriend stuff," you said. *Friends.* But she wanted to go with a boy who smelled like Old Spice, played football, grabbed her ass in front of people, and liberally used the word *faggot*.

Instead of going to the prom, you stayed home and listened to the Cure and Nine Inch Nails and wrote poetry about how no one understood you.

Are you here because it's so much better here than where you used to be? Because it's not a place where people whisper, point, and laugh? Call you things behind your back and fear you in the locker room when it's time to shower? Is here better than pretending to be okay with hateful conversations? Than pretending to come? Than pretending to be happy?

I know this questioning makes you lonely. When you refused to label yourself, that meant you had no community. Belonging is a beautiful thing, but you just decided it was better to go to the best parties and the fun meetings, and fuck labels.

You'd prefer not to think you are here because of who you decided to go to bed with yesterday, or the day before that, or the week before that. Maybe you're not here because of whom you decide to fuck. You are certainly not here because you changed your mind about who you wanted to fuck three, four, or seven times.

You are here because you finally realize that none of these things matter. If you're anything like me, people will ask you questions such as, "What's your sexual preference?" and "What are you, anyway?" And if you're anything like me, you won't ever have (or want to have) an answer.

You know whatever you say today might be different tomorrow, that you'll lust and long for someone new, and that will change what you thought you knew about who you are. That lust and longing will hit you fiercely, from what feels like nowhere, maybe at a dive bar after that fourth whisky shot, when a petite blonde in a slinky black dress tells you you're a fantastic dancer. Maybe it'll hit you when the pretty-boy barista with the asymmetrical haircut smiles at you and coyly tells you he loves Earl Grey tea too. Maybe it'll hit you when your beautiful butch friend pulls the chair out for you at dinner and calls you *ma'am*.

New yearnings will hit you like a fantastic fist, and your stomach will twist and your fingertips will burn and desire will be brand-new again. Over and over again. You may be here, and it may feel like you're lost in the middle of nowhere, but here you get to feel the newness of desire over and over again.

You'll never have to decide with finality what (or who) it is you desire. You just need to learn to enjoy that freedom to desire, despite all the questions from the people who are afraid. Tab A fits in Slot B, and that's the way it has to be? Fuck that. Fuck whoever you want, instead.

Today you are here. Yesterday you were there. Tomorrow, maybe, you'll be somewhere else. You've made it this far, but there's always so much more change for you. Chances are, this is going to make people uncomfortable. They'll be afraid of your fluidity, and they'll hate your happiness. Don't worry about it. They need maps. They need that tiny dot that proclaims location and definition, and they cling to it as if letting go will make the world fall apart.

You? The world will be yours.

# You Bear, Me Jane

## R.M. Vaughan

You are a bear. This did not happen by accident. You and a bunch of other large, hairy guys decided years ago that being run down and dismissed by mainstream gay culture solely because your body size does not match some marketing firm's idea of the "ideal gay male" was no longer a sustainable proposition. You rebelled. You celebrated your curves, your gorgeous bellies, your massive, furry sweater puppies, your eating habits.

You created a viable subculture, you learned to love yourselves. You made a place for fatties (like me), made me feel sexy again. I thank you.

But lately, my dear giant man, you've gotten a little, well, reactionary. Let's trace your problem back to the source: body size.

As you well know, being fat is now a sin in our culture. Fat equals stupid, fat equals lazy, fat equals weak, fat equals morally bankrupt (I could go on here, but you get the picture). Being fat means you always have to say you're sorry—sorry for taking up space, sorry for enjoying your food in public, sorry for not covering your body in a burlap sack, sorry for showing up at the bathhouse in a towel and not a burqa.

And, worse yet, for the muscles-and-abs set, your fat makes you something less than a man, makes your body softer and thus more feminine: fat makes your sweet, full-cheeked smile just a little too girlish for their hard, sterile tastes. In other words, fat equals female—not a turn-on for most gay men.

So, I understand why you, my good bear, have chosen to identify with all of the most conservative representations of male identity: the truck driver, the lumberjack, the construction worker, the cop/fireman/soldier. I understand how being told you are not manly would drive you to overcompensate. But, my dear friend, you've gone too far. You are now officially a boring straight guy. How is that revolutionary? How does that fix any of gay culture's body image stupidities or internalized homophobia? When have boring straight guys ever fixed anything?

You will say that I am just angry because I can't play the game, and you're half right. I can't. I won't even try anymore. I have worn the plaid sleeveless shirts and the camouflage cargo shorts, the big black cowboy belts and the regulation army boots ... and I looked like a half-formed F-to-M tranny, minus the sexual mystery or adventure, the glamor of difference. I looked like I was trying too hard, because I was. What can I tell you? I am fat, really fat, but I like bright colors and sparkles, scarves and cologne, and smart man-purses.

How you hated me, back in my faux bear days. How you hate me still. I remind you of that original insult (which, in truth, I never found all that insulting, because I like women, they're my friends), of being called a titty-boy sissy.

You are ashamed of the fact that, as far as most of society is concerned, your body still registers as weak, as a product of lack of self-control, no matter how hard you try to toughen up your aura with redneck cut-offs and leather bar T-shirts. And when your look failed to carry your message, you resorted to a more direct approach: You are now officially femme-phobic, even misogynist. You disappoint me, and I scare you.

When I see you on *bear411.com* or *bearforest.com* or *leather bear.com* and think you look sexy, I lose my urge when I see "no queens, no perfume, no flamers" in your profile. I hate to see you hating other gays.

Didn't you learn anything from being hated? Didn't you learn that stupid rules only make the world less fun? Didn't you learn that being gay is a blessing, and that everybody is entitled to his own gayness?

Fat gayness, hairy gayness, screaming high-toned, drag-queen gay-ness, dull middle-class, dog-walking, cooking-class gayness? Didn't being treated like shit teach you not to treat other people like shit?

I don't want to get all political, but you, my dear large man, need to consider the full consequences of your new machismo. You are one step away from being the same sort of man who used to beat up your gay ancestors.

You can look like a backwoods hooligan all you want (it's all drag, after all), but if you start thinking like one, thinking that girly gays are not your equals, that maleness has only one way of express-ing itself (i.e., your way), you're only helping the people who want to hurt us. Yes, "us." Your gay community. Please remember who your friends are and are not.

Those manly-men types, after whom you model your look—and now your worldview—will not come to your aid when the world turns on you again. I'll be there for you, even if I am angry with you right now. So be there for me, now. I am a fat gay guy who likes pretty things. You need to find room for me, too, because I am not going away any time soon, or getting any thinner.

Finally, my sweet and chubby pal, you know, in your clogged heart of hearts (I can say that because I also live on chips and pizza, and my heart stopped beating efficiently twenty years ago), that you don't really want to be a straight jerk.

You know that after you get home from "Big Boys Cigars and Boots Night" at The Pump or The Diesel or The Chrome Bar, af-ter you've parked your jeep (why do you own a jeep when you live downtown?) and fed your hunting dogs (same question) and checked your messages on *bigmusclebear.com*, you are going to watch re-runs of *Gilmore Girls*. You are going to eat cupcakes with sprinkles. You are going to worry that it might not rain enough for your azalea bushes. You are going to make a shopping list (white wine, skinless chicken breasts, asparagus, organic butter). You are going to put on slippers—comfy, plush slippers with velvety lining. You are going to let yourself be the gay man you are.

You don't want to hear this, but nobody buys the he-man routine. You couldn't fool the Pope with your "straight-acting" shtick. Your own mother wonders when you're going to stop dressing like somebody who skins road kill for shoe leather (she paid for your degree in medieval literature, after all). And you certainly don't fool me, because you and I have had some great sex, and I know that the thing you like the most is the cuddling.

So, you and I need to have dinner, we need to sit down and talk. You and I need to stop baiting each other (okay, I'll stop right after this letter). You and I need to forgive each other our particular indulgences (perfume for me, your habit of adding the word "bear" to every noun), and be gay men together. You and I need each other more than the world needs either of us.

Here's a deal: I'll cut down on the more flowery scents and try not to always wear matching Easter egg-colored socks and shirts, and, in turn, you will wash that filthy ball cap, the one that smells like a rotting goat.

I will try to smoke a cigar. You will borrow one of my wigs. We will be friends again. We will share the chips and dip.

# How to Label Yourself, or Not: Coming Out and Coming to Terms

## B.J. Epstein

So you've come out.

You're here, you're queer! You're loud, you're proud!

So how should you, or could you, label yourself? And why? There are so many possibilities to choose from: homosexual, bisexual, monosexual, gay, lesbian, transgender, queer, questioning, curious, genderqueer, transsexual, pansexual, omnisexual, pomosexual, intersex, open-minded, ambisexual, polyamorous, heterosexual-who-sometimes-likes-people-of-the-same-gender, polysexual, trisexual (or trysexual), asexual, fag, butch, femme, bear, dyke, fairy, master, slave, womyn, drag queen, and numerous other appellations. You can choose one or more of these labels, and you can buy the concomitant flags and jewelry, and go to the appropriate bars and clubs, and march in the right parades, and so on, but what is the point?

Now that you have finally admitted to yourself and others that you are not hetero, and now that you have gotten comfortable with that, you might feel you should advertise your status—wear a rainbow belt buckle or a bi-pride necklace or a pink triangle patch—or that you should tell anyone you meet that you are out. You don't want to hide or be ashamed anymore. You have probably struggled and suffered because of your sexuality and/or gender identity, and now you are ready to tell the world (or at least part of it) who you really are. You might even want to reclaim words that have been used pejoratively by people outside the community and infuse them with pride and strength. You may gravitate toward one or two terms and feel they identify you best: Maybe you're a butch lesbian or a bear-who-likes-hairless-guys, or you're a polyamorous trisexual, or perhaps a transgender queer. You know, or think you know, what those labels mean and how they relate to you. After what might have been years of questioning your sexuality, of not knowing who and what you were (or knowing but being unable to tell others), it can be a relief to have a name to call your own.

But what do people, whether in the LGBT community or not, really think when they hear the word "queer" or any of those other labels? Do they truly understand all that you feel goes into the label? And what do they think when they see your freedom rings or your bear beach towel? Do they recognize what you have gone through and all that your chosen label means to you? Or do they simply have stereotypical ideas about what a dyke or a fag is? Many people find comfort in labels and in the ability to box others into a particular category. Labels can be a lazy sort of shorthand, an easy way of thinking you know someone without having to do the actual work involved in getting to true knowledge. You might say, for example, "That's a black woman," and those two words, "black" and "woman," each create images and ideas in your head. Based on these ideas, you feel you can guess something about this person and her experiences and you may be right to some extent, but it is also quite possible that you are wrong. You probably don't bother to ask the person, because you already feel you know, just from the label, and all the associations that go with those words, a little about what it means for someone to be a black woman professor, or a gay Mexican Catholic, or a multilingual Eastern European businessman, or a monosexual atheist male-to-female, or a Jewish vegetarian writer.

Labels allow people to identify, but they also carry preformed ideas and judgments, both from within the queer community and outside it. If you call yourself a bisexual woman (or womyn), some lesbians scorn you—even reject you—as "on the fence" or "indecisive" or "someone who likes heterosexual privilege." Someone who is transgender and straight may be made to feel excluded from both the LGBT community (because she/he is, after all, straight) and the hetero one (because she/he does not have the simple gender identity people expect and prefer). Just when you think you're comfortable with your identity, others use those labels against you.

So this is the dilemma you face. You've worked hard to come to terms (both figuratively and literally) with your sexuality, and there is no need to lie or conceal it. But you want people to get to know the real you and not make assumptions that may be false. The question is, then, whether the real you is in fact encoded in the labels you use to describe yourself. And if it is, do others recognize and understand that? As a newly minted queer (or whatever you want to call yourself), you have every right to be proud of who you are and of all the experiences you have lived through. But you might want to consider what the labels mean and how they are used before you settle on a term (or two or three), because the very labels you think represent you may actually be misrepresenting you to others.

# Every Room After: Notes to Jean Genet

## Jason Timermanis

*Monstre sacré.* It's quite the label. The *sacred monster* of French literature. Who wouldn't wonder about such a designation?

Of course, there were all the other things they called you: thief, prostitute, pervert—but also romantic, intellectual, original. Twenty-two years after your death, however, what lingers in people's minds is *monstre sacré.*

Monsters are useful, after all. They clarify positions. Our own goodness is so much more distinguishable when evil rests on its haunches in a corner, easily pointed at. To be virtuous we just have to walk away from it, from you, our lips curled in disgust.

But as a writer, and therefore a communicator, you asked us through your books and plays to walk towards you, and I did. In a library, when I was seventeen, I came across you while discreetly searching the shelves for any book to better explain the gay world I was about to step into.

Instead, I found you.

I picked up your novel *Funeral Rites*, and the initial juxtaposition of the book's front and back covers was enough to grab my attention. Nazism, its brutal grim weight, dominated the front with a large black swastika, while on the back I found a description of one man's love affair with another. The crux of *Funeral Rites* is the extinguished relationship between two men, both named Jean. It's an elegy by one Jean in the wake of the other's death during World War II. Jean D. is a twenty-year-old French Resistance fighter in German-occupied Paris, whose death we read of from the novel's first page.

The book's narrator is you, Jean Genet, or some distortion of yourself masquerading under your real name. A mournful howl over dead love between men, the book is also a knife twist in the back of devotion. We know the soldier Jean D. spent his last days evading the Nazis. You write, "I myself brought the detectives to the apartment in which [Jean D.] was hiding, and I made a point of being paid off for my betrayal before his very eyes."

As a result of this betrayal, Jean D. is shot to death, and we're left as readers to reconcile the fact that you chose this; to be ravaged by grief, yet strangely, not by guilt. It was your own personal twist on the Christian ideal of suffering as noble and illuminating. By having Jean D. killed, you could see how down-to-the-bone your suffering went, and from it gauge how deep your love for him truly ran. You measured love by the length of its shadow.

You forced not only an unsettling morality upon the reader, but also a difficult take on gay love—as grimy and coarse, inseparable from death. Love and death are about devouring and being devoured. You wrote of Jean D.'s body:

> The bees escape from his eyes, from his sockets where
> the liquid pupils have flowed from under the flaccid
> eyelids. To eat a youngster shot on the barricades, to
> devour a young hero, is no easy thing. We all love the
> sun. My mouth is bloody. So are my fingers. I tore the
> flesh to shreds with my teeth.

It wasn't just the war, or betrayal, but love that reduced Jean D. to a thing metaphorically choked down. And it was a love never hung up on being gay love. Not apologetic. Not diminutive.

What if I was attracted to my own sex?

It's a complicated question we ask ourselves, one that can consume an entire life. You wrote often of men in prison cells, aware that the claustrophobia of the convict mirrors the social entombment of all gays. Queers make their own exits. We've had to carve them out of the rock, push through and into other rooms, poorly lit antechambers, where we can finally breathe. This self-exhumation is exhausting, and most of us spend our lives content with this first gulp of free air. Few keep digging for what could be beyond the next wall, or the next. You wrote:

> There are some homosexuals who wish to affirm their
> difference and their special quality, and this need
> leads them to unmask the arbitrary character of the
> system in which they live. But there are others who
> wish to pass unnoticed and to blend into the system,
> therefore strengthening the system.

What if I was attracted to my own sex?

If we can answer that first complicated question, we as queers can hopefully develop the mental fortitude and dexterity to ask other difficult questions, at first maybe sexual, but then expanding outward.

Are love and betrayal necessarily exclusive?

Why is one thing sacred and another monstrous?

What lives in the shadows of our common values, and are those things worthy of our love?

Each question we ask, no matter how ugly, is another opening in another wall. Normal isn't a location but the act of settling in a room; some do it for life, others for just a little while.

Jean, you never stayed long in any room, figuratively or literally. And your difficult questions, they led you further and further from conventional society:

> It was by raising to the level of virtue, for my own
> use, the opposite of the common virtues that I
> thought I could attain a moral solitude where I would

never be joined. I chose to be a traitor, thief, looter, informer, hater, destroyer, despiser, coward. With axe and cries I cut the bonds that held me to the world of customary morality. At times I undid the knots methodically.

I have never wanted to betray someone I love, but I thank you, Jean, for your own literary betrayals. They've illuminated what lies miles out from the conventional. I may not venture all the way to that edge with you, but your light has revealed the vast space that is possibility. Without you I might have just stayed in a room of someone else's making, thinking walls were just walls and not things to be broken through.

Monstrosity is relative. You're a reminder that the simple admission of being gay was, and in some circles still is, monstrous. You've taught me that there can be beauty in the dark, in what is ugly, and that ugly is often just a question unasked.

# To My Sisters and Brothers in Hiding

## Roz Kaveney

You wouldn't call it hiding, of course. You would call it stealth, as if that made a difference.

But it doesn't. Not really.

You call it stealth, and that sounds like something high-tech and clever. You call it hiding, and it sounds a bit less grand.

You call it stealth, and it sounds like you are walking in dangerous woods so lightly that not a twig crunches beneath your perfectly pedicured feet; you call it hiding, and it is too much like hiding under the bedclothes or in a closet.

A different closet, of course.

You call it stealth, and it is a piece of cleverness to be proud of. You call it hiding, and it sounds like shame.

So you call it stealth.

And you talk, some of you, as if it were the only true and proper way for all trans women and trans men to lead our lives. You talk as if your choices were the only authentic way to live a transsexual existence, as if those trans folk who make other choices are doing it wrong, are pathetic failures.

And some of you call it Harry Benjamin's Syndrome, just as a way of being super-special, and not just ordinary transsexuals like the rest of us.

You talk as if it were your own idea, rather than something that doctors and social workers told you that you ought to want to do. Maybe it has become your own idea, by now, the way most things we are talked into do, after a while.

They taught you shame, and you learned to think of that shame as self-respect. They told you there was only one sort of acceptance possible; that the only way society could tolerate the outward manifestation of your inner and unchanging gender was if you never, ever admitted your history.

Of course, there are parts of the world where this is true, places where any variation from the norm leads to villagers with torches and pitchforks, leads to the rope and the flame.

There is self-protection; there is prudence; there is not volunteering for martyrdom.

You think, some of you, that society cannot bear much reality, that you have to be just like everyone else, that you have to hide in total conformity with their rules. What is wrong is to turn the necessity for self-protection into a philosophical position, to say that the peasants and the witch burners and the storm troopers have a point.

Anne Frank hid in her attic for as long as she could, but she did not call her attic stealth.

Most of you, though, are not in any imminent danger of death, or at least no more than anyone else in this violent world. Most of you live safe middle-class suburban lives, not that different from a lot of other trans people who make different choices.

Not everyone lives in stealth, but a lot of trans people lead quiet lives nonetheless.

You have not, in the end, all that much to be afraid of.

It is other people who have to be afraid.

There are young trans women and men out there who are not leading safe, middle-class suburban lives. Some of them are homeless, and some of them are whores, and some of them take half-baked risks on dates with dangerous men.

A lot of them had to drop out of schools that were not all that good to begin with, and a lot of them were cast aside by families who had beaten them, and many of them were already victims of a society that oppresses on grounds of race and class.

And most of that did not happen to you, and most of that did not happen to me.

Some of them die.

Some of them die because the dangerous men found out who they were, and some of them die because the dangerous men did not.

Dangerous men kill women, and dangerous men kill cute boys, too.

That is why they are dangerous.

Some of you—some is not polite code for most—talk about those dead young women and men as if they had failed.

As if they had died for failing in a game in which they never had the choice to play, by rules they never got to know or make or cast aside. They made, not your choices, but those of people whose choices are limited, and some were bad choices. But not ones they made because they were wrong or stupid.

They were your sisters and your brothers.

Some of you spit in their dead faces. And you do not understand why those who care about those dead kids, your sisters and your brothers, get vexed with you, why you get up people's noses by sticking your noses in the air.

Some of you feel that stealth does not apply to the Internet, and you tell anyone who is watching precisely what you think of those trans folk whose choices are not yours.

You have nothing but contempt for those trans women and trans men who lead their lives in the open, for whom getting acceptance from society is not about pretending they don't exist, who would rather change the world than be changed by it. Trans women and trans men who are brave and strong and free, who are singers and writers and campaigners.

Pathetic failures, one of you said.

Because, of course, real women live in the suburbs, real women are hockey moms, and real trans women live in the suburbs and drive their adopted kids to hockey and everything is hunky-dory for them.

Which is absolutely fine for those of you who want to live that life, and a perfectly fine life it is, too. Right up to the moment when you think it is the only life anyone should want and spit in the faces of those who reject it.

One of the things about singing and writing is that you need an audience. As an artist, you are pursuing excellence in what you do, and that means putting all of yourself into your work, and that means all of your history, too. Some of your audience is going to be smart, close readers and listeners, and there is no way that you can hide from your audience.

One of the things about campaigning is that you cannot lie, because lies multiply. You have to be unashamed because shame will bring you down in the end; it's never the crime, it's always the cover-up that destroys political lives and the causes that those lives serve.

You may feel no urge to create or change minds; you may feel we get what we want in life; you may feel that remaking one's existence so that it is authentic for the first time is enough creation for one lifetime. And you are entitled to feel all those things.

But you are not, any of you, entitled to tell other people that their choices are wrong, that their choices make them pathetic failures. You don't get to do that. You have no patent on the transsexual identity and no claim to tell other trans folk what to do.

Oh, you say, but people who don't live in stealth are just vulgar exhibitionists whom other people see as a freak show. As if there were anything wrong with exhibitionism or being a freak, because some of the best and truest artists and sages in this world are exhibitionists and freaks, and not just those who are trans. Remember Socrates?

Yes, you say, and look what happened to him.

You assume is that living in the open is living with your past on perpetual display—and here's the thing. In a world where people are interested in art or other sorts of excellence, an artist's personal history is of interest, but not as much as their art or other forms of excellence.

In a world where the highest value is a perfectly turned couplet or a brilliant string of logic, the fact that one used to have a dick and now has a cunt, or vice versa, is not something that is politely ignored, but it is not of the greatest interest, either.

It may be different in the suburbs. It may be that when considering the best possible flan, or the perfectly ordered garden, such other details are considered crucial. You would know better than the rest of us about that. But, you say, by being open, trans folk who are not interested in "passing," as an absolute value, are a threat to the rest of the community. People can watch and learn from them and learn how to decode the secrets of people who live in stealth. It's not just that the noisy ones give those who are quiet a bad name; it is that there is something specific in the noise they make which unlocks that quietness and strips naked those comfortable suburban lives.

There seems to be an element of magical thinking in all of this, an idea that stealth has to be universal, like the sleep of those in Sleeping Beauty's kingdom, or the universal admiration of the Emperor's new clothes. A fear that a few trans people who march to a different drum will unravel things for the rest of you.

Oh, and then there is the lesbian thing and the gay thing and the LGBT thing and the queer thing and the genderqueer thing.

Not all of you are straight, of course, but those of you who are lesbian and gay tend to be those things in a desperately assimilationist suburban way.

A lot of you, though, really don't like the T being on the end there, or anywhere near the L and the G. Those of you whose self-respect looks a little bit like shame tend to be desperately antsy about the rest of us going to Pride.

Of course, things may go badly wrong for everyone down the line, and the trains will come and take the L and the G away, and the B and the T as well. And you will not be safe on that day, so you may as well accept that life out here in the minorities is awfully unprotected without a bit of solidarity.

And the fact that some gay men and lesbians have been or still are complete jerks to trans people should not stand in the way of acknowledging that you and they have the same enemies.

You don't want to listen to us say that, do you?

You think our saying that is just us causing trouble. Which, of course, gives you a set of perfect scapegoats when things go badly for you individually, as sometimes they will. And none of which would have happened without the bad transsexuals spoiling it for the good, the perfect, the authentically true, the utterly transitioned ones.

When things go bad for you, out there in the suburbs—when messy divorce leaves you out in the open, without custody of your children, or bereavement leaves you stripped of inheritance rights and your suburban friends—who is going to care for you?

Some of you will cluster around and put friendship before anonymity—of course you will, because most of you are nice people and only a few of you spew hateful crap—but, mostly, living in stealth means living without other trans people in your lives.

Why would you want to know each other when you are no more alike, save for this one fact you wish to set aside, than you are like the woman next door and the woman next door to her?

So, who will campaign for your rights? Who will express solidarity and try to dry your tears?

Oh, that would be those pathetic failures who campaign and write and sing. And bite their lips about past insults, because solidarity—when you feel it—is inalienable, and a trans woman whom suburban life has chewed up and spat out is as much a sister as a homeless kid selling herself on the street.

You may not feel that we are your sisters and brothers, but we are, worse luck for all of us.

Yours in sisterly love and some envy for your happy delusions,
    Roz

# How to Hate Yourself Completely

Natty Soltesz

Start by standing in front of the mirror. It's important to free your mind, so think: Your body could be better—you should work out. Then know: If you joined a gym, you'd stay motivated for a week—a month, tops—and then you'd quit. So why bother?

Teeth could be whiter. Cock could be bigger. Beyond that, though, study your mannerisms. Slight lisp? Short stride? Hair too perfect or not perfect enough?

All of these things are important, especially if you want to get laid, and surely you do—you're gay. You're sex-obsessed and you fuck indiscriminately. And even if you aren't fucking anybody, you're surely *thinking* about it.

Remember this around relatives, workmates, people with small children. Nephews, young students—boys who are just beginning to bloom. Their parents know what you're thinking. You can't wait to get your hands on that impressionable flesh; you want to pound it into submission, so it's soft, malleable, ready to be molded into a replica of yourself.

The gay agenda has little to do with social acceptance or pride—it's about sex. Pure selfish hedonism. To you, morality is a thing of the past.

You probably have HIV (don't even *try* to pretend it's something other than a gay disease), which you contracted despite the fact that it's completely preventable. You probably have genital warts and herpes and are on your fifth round of crabs. This is par for the course. Let's just come out and say it: You deserve it.

Why? (You've got to be kidding me.) Because you weren't careful enough. Because you don't have self-control. Because you can't admit your culpability.

Maybe you're a self-identified bisexual, or worse, you label yourself "queer." Give it up, this notion that sexuality is fluid, or permits a plethora of activity outside the bonds of standard, binary forms of attraction. You're a faggot. Own up to it.

Of course, if you like to fuck other guys, it's not the act itself that's turning you on, other than the satisfaction you get from symbolically possessing masculine aspects that you've denied in yourself. (For this we can surely blame your father, who never taught you to play baseball.)

Hey, maybe you and I can devise some semblance of a relationship and pretend that we're in love? Maybe this will provide a brief respite from the crushing knowledge that we are, in fact, über-narcissistic men-children, forever slaves to a thumb-sucking mommy complex, destined to die in loneliness and despair because we can never love anyone as much as we love ourselves?

Anyway, we won't bother with condoms. Do you really, ahem, respect yourself enough to try and protect yourself from a disease that—heaven forefend—you don't already possess?

Please. Surely anyone would consider it an honor to receive an STD that might hasten their departure from a world in which they attempt to normalize behaviors that are obviously unnatural, a world in which they exhibit a denial bordering on psychosis, a world in which they do not see that men were given a penis and women a vagina for a reason, a world in which homosexual behavior violates the very fabric of human existence and the universe. Sex isn't supposed to be fun.

But you willfully ignore this and go on with your fetishist and sadomasochistic games. Sure, tell yourself that you're only role-playing, when deep inside you know that the very things that turn you on are a mirror of your hatred for yourself. You want to get slapped around because you deserve to be slapped around—you want to be punished for the sinful life you've chosen (yes, chosen) for yourself. You fetishize straight guys, masculine guys, because in your heart you know that that's what you're supposed to be.

So go ahead—cum. Enjoy that fleeting moment of pleasure.

Isn't it depressing to think of all that you've just wasted? Instead of taking part in the beautiful creation of life, you've resigned yourself to a state of suspended adolescence in which you espouse the futile and vile notion that the gay "lifestyle" is somehow "normal" and "acceptable."

Your precious seed of life has become little more than excrement, to be eventually shat out of one's bowels and cast into the sewer, the sewer where our kind most assuredly belongs.

But then you already knew this, all of this, and more.

Getting Your Queer On

# Why You *Should* Have Sex on the First Date

Steven Bereznai

I have read a lot of gay dating books, a *lot* of them. I am a junkie. And one thing they all seem to agree on is that if you want to find a boyfriend you should not, I repeat, *not* have sex on the first date. They go further. No sex for the first *three* dates. I have followed this advice on several occasions, and I have to tell you, it just does not work for me. And it's not just me; I've talked with many gay men about this and discovered that, for some of us, the "wait and see before having sex" approach works about as well as the rhythm method of birth control.

So, why do so many "experts" recommend the three-date technique? Why doesn't it achieve the intended results for me and many other gay men? What are the potential emotional consequences of sleeping with a guy on the first date? And the hardest question: how can I deal with those consequences in a healthy way?

For the purpose of this advice, consider meeting a guy in a bar your first date. After all, it *is* a common way for gay men to make new acquaintances, and we otherwise are often faced with the question, "Do I take him home now or wait for a date?" (Make that three dates, if you follow the advice of the dating books.)

My bottom line is that if you want to see this guy again (whether you've met at a bar or on a more conventional first date), then go ahead and have sex. If you're not sure, by all means go on another date to get some clarity. In my experience, however, if I don't have sex with a guy right away, I'm not having sex with him at all.

*One Night Stands Can Become Long-term Relationships*
Let's recap what's already being said in favor of the straightaway hookup.

- If there's no sexual chemistry/compatibility between the sheets, you might as well find out sooner
rather than later.
- The total hottie loophole: You don't know when a
guy this sizzling is going to come your way again,
so get it while the getting's good, 'cause your first
date with him may be your last. If you're going to
let a god slip through your fingers, it better be with
lots and lots of lube. Finally, there's the excuse of
general horniness/sluttiness clouding your judgment
and rendering you incapable of waiting for three
dates.

And yet, the gay relationship books argue that all of the above should take a back seat to the three-date rule for those who are serious about getting into an LTR—a long-term relationship. Wrong, wrong, wrong. Okay, right, right, right for *some* people. Not me. Maybe not for you. As the British *Queer as Folk* puts it, "That was the night he came along, the one-night stand that never went away." In other words, sex on the first date *can* lead to an LTR. Heck, I know a couple who met in a bathhouse. Not only did they have sex on the first "date," one of them had already had sex with two other guys that night. All the same, here they are, a couple of decades, several dogs and cats, and a bed and breakfast later, still together.

*Why the Gay Dating Books Think You Should Wait*
Why are the gay dating books so hell-bent on the three-date rule? On closer examination, it has less to do with the actual guy you are

with at the moment and more to do with the dating process in general. The experts make a pretty fair assumption that, in your quest for "the one," you are going to go on dates with a *lot* of different guys. This can be a draining and emotional process.

When you finally meet someone you are really into, it's natural to want to get sexual with him ASAP. The books say to hold off because, if you do have sex with him, and it turns out to be a one-night stand, the emotional fallout for you can be pretty devastating and demoralizing. Repeat the cycle too often, and presto, you've got a classic case of bitter queenitis; once the syndrome becomes chronic, good luck finding an LTR after that.

The three-date rule is intended to be a buffer to prevent repetitive stress injury (for those of us who have experienced the syndrome, this is not just a cute metaphor). In theory, if you like a guy and he doesn't get back to you after the first or second date, the sense of rejection will be less charged if you haven't had sex. This leaves you more grounded and more open to the next guy who comes along. So, waiting until after three dates is the romantic equivalent of getting an ergonomic computer mouse to prevent carpal tunnel syndrome.

*Why Waiting Fails Many Gay Men*
If you've already tried the three-date method and found it's the way to go for you, bravo! But this method did not work for me.

Contrary to what my friends, books, and pop culture once led me to believe, it's not because I'm a total slut, nor is it because I'm a hunter constantly in need of further conquests; and it's not because all I'm interested in is a guy's body—not that I'm saying there's anything wrong with any of the above. I've been a slut, a hunter, and I've definitely got a superficial bone or two in my body. All the same, that's not what was holding me back.

The truth is, like many gay men, I have a lot of anxiety.

There, I said it.

I know what some of you are thinking. If I patiently get through three dates, I will start to feel more comfortable—less anxious—with the other person. I'll get to know the person better, we'll have easier conversations and build inside jokes, we'll cuddle on the couch while we watch *Heroes* or *Ugly Betty*. But the longer I wait to have sex with a guy, the more intimidating the thought becomes. It builds and builds in importance. It takes on mythic proportions. In other words, I psyche myself out. One time, I started dating a guy and insisted we wait until after the third date to have sex. Five weeks and twenty dates later, we still hadn't done the deed. There was lots of making out, grinding on the dance floor while Justin Timberlake brought sexy back, and plenty of under-the-sweater action. But by the third and fourth dates there wasn't enough booze in the world to calm me down enough to go all the way. Suffice it to say, we broke up.

Of course, one solution would be to work on reducing my anxiety as I get to know someone. But here's the thing: I've found a much more efficient way of addressing the situation.

Have sex right away.

I've met guys who are even more anxious than I am. There was, for example, the giggler. I assumed he was just high, because he kept having little laughing fits while we were making out. But no, once we got naked and really fired up, his giggling was replaced by noises of a rather different, and more gratifying, nature. Do you really think, had we waited, that we'd have made it through three whole dates and then had sex? Considering our combined anxiety, I highly doubt it. One or both of us would have found a reason to flake out.

And it would have been a real shame if I had missed the chance to have the fun that we did. That first date was on my birthday, and birthday sex *rocks*. Don't pass it up for three dates that may go nowhere!

*Things Will Not Always Go Well*

Of course, for every happy story, there's a not-so-happy story, and anxiety can get the better of a gay man in ways that are not as benign as a bit of nervous laughter. In one case where I brought a guy home right away, he wound up asking me to stop while I was blowing him because he was so nervous. He was totally shaking.

Some of you might be thinking that he's a prime example of someone who *should* wait three dates before having sex. You may be right. And I was respectful about pulling off of him. We exchanged digits, chatted for a while, and agreed to go for a walk in a few days. It would have been lovely—except he never called me back. I was hurt, rejected, and confused, but ultimately I figured he was just not that into me. I refused to contemplate the possibility that I was really bad at giving head. And with good reason. A month later Halloween rolled around and he came running up to me amidst the ghoulish gay goblins on Toronto's über-gay Church Street. He chatted me up for almost an hour. On the one hand I was annoyed (who did this guy think he was?); on the other, it made me feel less self-conscious that he'd asked me to take my mouth off his dick.

I encouraged him to call. Once again, he didn't.

I am convinced he'd have done us both a real service by having sex with me the first time. Granted, I should've gone a little more slowly than unzipping his fly and going down on him while he was still fully dressed. Live and learn, girls, live and learn. But the idea of waiting for an actual date (let alone three) wasn't going to make it any easier for him.

*The Dark Side of the Three-Date Excuse*

Which brings me to the Darth Vader section of the no-sex-for-three-dates philosophy.

While some gay men genuinely believe in waiting, others abuse the three-date rule, myself included. Sometimes when a guy says,

"Let's wait," he really means, "Let's wait forever." In fact, this is probably the only time that I like to use the three-date rule. It's the perfect out, and I get to hide behind a false virtue. My friends will be totally rooting for a particular guy, and I'll tell them that I'm waiting three dates before having sex. Then I make sure to cut it off at two (or better yet, one). Look at me, I'm such an evolved gay man, so much better than the guys who get it on right away and then never talk to each other again.

That was sarcasm. If you're going to use the three-date rule, try to use it with integrity, and if you know you're not sexually interested in someone, it's okay to be honest about it. (Steven Bereznai, this means you!)

### The Post-Orgasm Meltdown

There is just one last thing I have to say about having sex on the first night, and I've intentionally saved it until the end because I think it's the most important. What happens when you have sex right away, you fall for the guy, and you're totally crushed when he never calls you back?

Let me tell you about "Eric." If I'd followed the three-date rule, I know for a certainty we would never have had sex, and that would be one of the great tragedies of my life. And there's nothing more painful than regret.

Eric was muscular, handsome, funny, smart, and charming. He was also really anxious. Giving him a massage worked wonders at calming us both down. And after he left the next morning, I was totally on cloud sixty-nine.

We spoke on the phone a few times after that. When he said he was staying in to watch a movie with some friends, I waited for him to invite me along. He didn't. During another conversation, when I suggested we meet for coffee, his response was, "Yeah, let's keep that in mind."

Ouch.

During Pride a few weeks later, I was hung over, and bawled during the Metropolitan Community Church open air service where the reverend spoke about the "Rainbow People" and how some kids couldn't hide the fact that they were different from other girls and boys. Elementary- and high-school memories poured out through my salty tears.

By the time I ran into Eric at the beer gardens a few hours later, I was serotonin-deprived and emotionally overwrought. I barked something bitchy at him. He gave me an unimpressed look and avoided me thereafter.

It was a defining moment. After all, I was no longer some doe-eyed ingénue torturing myself over crush after unattainable crush. I was now in my early thirties, and these churning feelings over Eric made me feel like I'd taken a major step back.

The three-date rule certainly would have spared me this.

It would also have robbed me of sex with one of the hottest guys I've ever been with and deprived me of the almost hypnotic experience of seducing him.

Was this to be my fate every time I had a one-night stand I hoped would blossom into something more? Would I totally snap and replay the events of our tryst over and over in my mind, trying to figure out where I went wrong, and assuring myself that if I could only trick him into getting to really know me he'd fall head over heels for me? And where did all that pent-up craziness come from?

The latter has proven to be the real question. I went to a therapist for months and months. Not to get over Eric. That took years, darling, and not without good reason. In therapy, I explored the coping mechanisms of my youth, which helped me survive my closeted years as an obvious and effeminate Rainbow Child in grade school and high school.

Like many gay men, that younger version of me learned to suppress my feelings. That helped me survive the closet, but it did not serve me quite as well when I was an adult gay man searching for intimacy. I was used to burying feelings, but every now and then I'd meet a guy like Eric who stirred them up, and my emotions would refuse to be buried. I'd never developed healthier ways of dealing with the anxiety that came exploding up after being rejected like that, and so with Eric, I flipped out.

Eric was not, in the end, just a one-night stand, and he's helped me to better understand myself. He was an opportunity for growth—at least that's what I made him, which is more than I can say for a lot of the guys I've gone on three dates with. He'll never be my boyfriend, but his memory will always have a small place in my big gay heart. And let's remember, the three-date rule isn't about getting a boyfriend, it's about insulating your heart while you search for "the one."

I like my way better.

# How to Date a Married Man

## Lewis DeSimone

I almost titled this essay "How *Not* to Date a Married Man." That might have been easier—and my advice would save you a lot of grief.

I could spend pages on how to spot married men: On the first date, for example, go to his house and search for clues—two sizes of shirts in the closet, two toothbrushes on the sink, slippers on both sides of the bed. Another fail-safe idea: Call his home phone when you know he's at work to hear how many names are on the machine's outgoing message. (If he refuses to give you his home phone number, that's a dead giveaway.) Or just try to trip him up: In the middle of a flowing conversation about movies, ask what his husband's favorite film is.

I could have made it all so simple: Don't date a married man, I might say (as if it were that easy). If he's in an open relationship, I'd tell you, then sure, you can sleep with him. But don't fall in love. Don't have romantic dinners and make out in the back row at the movies. Don't make him mix tapes and fantasize about him when you're sitting alone in your studio apartment and he's having a dinner party with the hubby. Don't do what I did. Don't put your life on hold because he can't stand the thought of you with another man. For heaven's sake, he goes home to another man every night.

But that's not what this essay is about. It's not as if you're seeking a married man. Who in his right mind would go looking for something he can't have? Lord knows I didn't look for an unavailable man. I just had one thrust upon me, so to speak. And I couldn't help myself.

So let's assume you've met him by accident. And you've gotten to know him by virtue of being thrown together by circumstances beyond your control. You work together, or you have mutual friends who always invite you to the same parties. You can't ignore the guy just because he's married; that would be rude. And chemistry is a powerful thing: You smell something in his hair that compels you; your body goes limp when he looks at you with those baby blues; his laughter is like Mozart in your ears. For better or worse, you're in love. Let's assume it's already gone too far.

If you're going to actually do something about it, the first thing to remember is to maintain some sort of control over your expectations. He's not going to leave his husband for you. Married men never do, especially if they've been together for a while and you're a young stud with little relationship experience. Asking him to leave his stable lover for you is rather like asking him to get out of his four-wheel-drive vehicle in a snowstorm and ride a ten-speed bike on the freeway instead. It might be fun for a while, but he knows he's not going to get where he needs to go, and he'll probably break a few ribs in the process.

Okay, so you've got realistic expectations. You might be in love, but you're not fantasizing about the white picket fence and attending PTA conferences together. Great.

The next thing you need to understand is a little trickier and perhaps a bit of a shock to your ego: He may love you, but he also loves his husband, and in a very different way. He's not looking for someone to give him exactly what his husband gives him. He's with you for something else, and it's not the way you cook or how clean you keep the house. Take that, together with the fact that your infrequent rendezvous lead to a strong build-up of lust, and the obvious can't be ignored. Even if he loves you, the primary function of your relationship is erotic, at least as far as he's concerned. And you'd better have the same priority, or you're going to be in deep trouble. Sure, you can strew rose petals on the bed and put some Norah Jones on the stereo, but this is not a romance. I hate to beat a dead horse, but this point cannot be made strongly enough: This is not a romance. You can kiss him from head to toe and whisper sweet nothings in his ear all night long, but what this really comes down to is two bodies coming together for a little passionate entertainment. You're not the love of his life; he's found that already. You're a charming guy he likes to be with, and you're a good lay. End of story.

Once you've come to terms with that, the next part should be a breeze. Remember to be discreet. You have to get used to the idea that your relationship will take place mostly behind closed doors. You won't be strolling down the red carpet together or attending the office Christmas party on his arm. If you do go out to dinner, there will be no handholding over the table, no French kiss goodnight on the sidewalk. People he knows could walk by at any moment—and when they do, you suddenly become a business associate or a long-lost cousin from Alberta.

You can't announce your love in the classifieds or shout it from the proverbial rooftops. Even telling your friends may be somewhat risky: The best ones will silently listen, waiting for you to come to your senses; the rest will scream at you to wake up and smell the mochaccino. You may get sympathy, but only for so long. Unless you want to double the masochism, you're probably better off keeping it to yourself.

Love is one of those things that no amount of logic can control. Your friends can't talk you out of it, only time can do that. Which brings us to the next rule of thumb: Accept your lover as he is.

The biggest mistake any of us make in relationships is thinking we can change the other person. You can't—least of all when your lover is a married man. The mere fact that he's with you is enough for him to handle. He knows he's breaking the rules just by being in your bed. Don't ask him to change his behavior outside of it.

To combat the guilt, he will hold his other principles even closer. If he's a Jet Li fan, don't expect him to watch a chick flick just because you're in the mood for a little Meg Ryan. If he's an opera queen, don't think you can broaden his horizons by using Madonna as mood music for your lovemaking.

You can, of course, use this to your advantage—not in a vindictive way, but as a reminder to take care of yourself. Your married man is a fragile soul. He's conflicted by his own behavior and terrified of being exposed. So don't make the mistake of putting him on a pedestal. Don't envy him, and don't feel jealous of his husband. Remember, the husband doesn't have what he thinks he has, or you wouldn't be in the picture at all.

Above all, respect yourself. Respecting yourself means minimizing the damage. It means drawing boundaries to define what you will and will not accept. Ultimately, it means knowing when to leave.

Let me share my experience with you. The first man I ever fell in love with was already taken, but that didn't stop me. I was head over heels for him. The moment I realized how I felt was life changing. Looking into his eyes, I not only fell in love, but also plummeted out of the closet. At that moment, the inner conflict I'd lived with for years (the voice that kept telling me my feelings for men were just a phase) dissolved. Instantly, I knew with absolute certainty not only that I was in love with the man before me, but also that I would never feel that way for a woman. I was free at last.

So free that I stepped out of one closet and into another. I began an affair with this man, my salvation, my gay messiah. And because he was already in a relationship—a decidedly closed one—I couldn't share the news. If I was going to have even a piece of him—even the occasional midweek dinner and a quick roll in the hay—I had to keep my mouth shut. And, despite being fresh out of the closet, I couldn't explore my sexuality with anyone but him. I couldn't go to bars, I couldn't make friends with other gay men, because all of that was a threat to our relationship. It was perfectly acceptable for my lover to have sex with two men, but I could have only him.

But I loved him, so I pretended to understand. I put his feelings ahead of mine. After all, he was older, he was established in his life, he was mature. He belonged on a pedestal. I told myself I should be glad for whatever fragments of his time and his life I could lay hold of, whatever crumbs he dropped on my plate.

It took a long time to turn my attention from him to me—to recognize that loving him was tantamount to not loving myself. Eventually, I broke it off. I discovered the joys of bachelorhood. But to be honest, despite all the men since then, I've never been able to recreate the feeling that memories of him still conjure in my heart. I've never since loved with that intensity.

His unavailability (spiced up with a pinch of my naïveté) is the main reason for that. I still fantasize about him because our relationship was never allowed to evolve beyond the fantasy stage. It was never tested in the real world—grocery shopping, paying the bills, listening to the minutiae of each other's day, crying on each other's shoulder about dreams unfulfilled.

And so we come to the final lesson: If you stumble into an impossible relationship—as most of us do at one time or another, whether the beloved is legally unavailable or only emotionally—just remember that it's not the end of the world. Do not define yourself by what you don't have, only by what you do with the lessons you learn.

You never know where the important lessons of life are going to come from. Sometimes he's shorter than you, sometimes freakishly taller. Sometimes he's wearing a cock ring, sometimes a wedding ring. In any case, keep your heart open so it can grow. And if it breaks a little now and then, it just learns to beat more strongly.

# How to Conjure Dead Poets

Julie R. Enszer

Allen Ginsberg said he could trace his seminal lineage to Walt Whitman, lover by lover by lover, all the way back until, somehow, the jism of Whitman was spilling on Ginsberg. You must do the same. *What lips my lips have kissed and where and why.* Trace your lesbian life from the tips of your fingers as they press inside a woman to reach back. Hacker, Lorde, Grahn, Sarton, Rukeyser, Taggard, Lowell, Stein, Vivien, Dunbar, Grimké, Dickinson. Reach further and further back, trusting there is a connection to Sappho, the tenth muse from the Island of Lesbos. Reach to her as Ginsberg reached to Whitman, while Whitman reached back to Greece. Trace your queer being backward through time. Reach out to the thousands of other queers who have lived and loved before you. Find them, hear them, embrace them. As you do, you are finding yourself. Your voice. You are affirming your lineage in a queer cultural heritage. You are surrounding yourself with them and letting them surround you. You embrace them; they, you. This is what you must do.

It is not easy. Our forbears are obscured. In elementary school, they teach us Whitman as an American bard and Dickinson as a crazy lady in white. They do not tell us of their homo-affections, their homoeroticisms, of their inferred, implied, and assured homosexualities, which they erase, elide, and deny. But they do teach us. They teach us how to find queer Walt and Emily on our own. They give us the tools to read beyond their proscriptions. We can read beyond what I am, you shall become, beyond kind Death stopping. Find Calamus, Whitman's ode to his ever-present erection. Find Emily's letters to beloved female intimates. Find these words urgently. Make them your own.

Always remember, they teach us how to read for their purposes, not for our own. Letters build words, words combine to build sentences. Sentences etch out thoughts, theories, conclusions. They teach us to read to teach us to live—but using their models. Citizens in a burnished democracy. Workers in the system of capitalism. Heterosexuals for hegemonic reproduction. This is the truth. You do not have to participate. You can resist.

Resistance begins in your own mind. A book. Or two. Discovered letters. Censored poems. A journal. A novel. Any could be your treasure trove. Begin by reading outside the dominant paradigm, or inside but in the closets, the cracks, the crevices. Gather candles or penlights, torches or lamps. Bring light to darkened pages, thought to old phrases. Even though they did not teach you about all the queers writing lyrics for their "best friends" or "intellectual companions" or telling encoded stories of their lives, there they dwell, in books, in libraries. On the pages, between the sheets. Their books are there. They have been waiting just for you. Read. Much has been written. There is much to understand.

Then, when you have filled your eyes, and they have settled into your mind, speak to them. Yes, it will be odd, at first, talking to dead poets. The oddness will abate as you spend more time alone, reading. To begin, you may carry on the conversation only in your mind. Staccato exchanges for you alone. Eventually, emboldened, you'll speak aloud. They will talk back. Fragments of their words, memorized, infused into your consciousness, will spill from your lips, the conversation flowing naturally and filling the quiet room of your body. These poets and writers are powerful companions. Imagine their bodies, their mouths, their tongues, their lips forming new words, words they have never written in sequences, words not yet thought. Let them tell you everything they have learned; what they've learned in life and since life passed from them. Listen. Then talk to them. They can be your best friends, your most intimate lovers. They will not betray you. They will never disappoint you. Every day, greet them anew. Reread their words; update them on your life.

At first, this must be your secret. The pleasure of these personal sojourns with our icons may be misunderstood by others with neither the time nor the inclination to pursue such mindful pleasures. Give your time, your mind, to the books and their preternatural companions.

There are others like you. Living. Today. Behind each lonely book on your library's shelf—a world of readers of today and long past. You'll see the smudges of their fingers on particular pages, the dog-ear to remember an apt turn of phrase, the bookmark buried inside for a poem to return. Call them to you, too.

Claim your people, living and dead. Gather them around your body and mind. Some may deny you the poets and writers and artists you claim for us queers, may chafe at the facts you've uncovered about their affections, may defend their false identities. Others may suggest "universal" frameworks in the poetry, finding shreds of evidence to bolster stories of heterosexuality. Listen to them. We have nothing to fear. You may smile and dismiss them. You may seek to convince them. You may respond or retreat. You may argue or upbraid. Whatever you do, speak your truth. Don't disappoint the specters around you.

As your ghostly friendships settle in, you must take their words and make them new. When the cacophony of their voices reaches a piercing din, you must silence them. Beg for a reprieve. Tell them that you love them, that you will always be here to listen, but for a spell, you must work in silence. Let them watch. When they wish, let them guide your pen. Write until you have no more. When your ink runs dry, bring them back in.

Now, it is time to tell everyone about your words, the books you've read—your people, your friends. Tell the eight-year-old memorizing

Dickinson, the adolescent reading Whitman. You have your voice, you have your conjuring skills. Make us a world with a queer genealogy so that some day you and all these ghosts may rest, thoughtfully and quietly, openly and honestly, within all the pages of the book of life.

# How to Be a Happy Slut
# (Five Easy Steps to Gay Whoredom)

Sky Gilbert

### 1. *Understand Who You Are*

When do you truly understand that you are a slut? It happens at different times for different people. I learned the truth from one of my best friends when I was a little more than thirty years old. I had moved into a house in Toronto with a bunch of self-confessed queers. I finally got up the courage to have a heart-to-heart chat with the notorious S&M dyke who lived upstairs. Her name was Sue Golding. After hearing the story of my life (I've always been a confessor; I usually give it up in the first ten minutes!), Sue declared, "You're a pervert." I was offended at first, until she explained that this was a compliment. "Being a pervert means that you like sex a lot, and you're not afraid to go out and pursue it as often as you like."

Hopefully, I will be your Sue Golding. If you are a slut, this may be the first time anybody identified who you are and told you it was okay to be that way. How do you know you're a slut?

First of all, ask yourself: "Is sex an important aspect of my life? Perhaps *the* most important? While others may have hobbies such as stamp collecting or making model airplanes, is my hobby sex?" It's likely that you usually prefer your sex separate from romance, and with a lot of different people in a lot of different ways. You think about sex a whole bunch, get horny a lot, and go out to the bar, baths, toilet, park, coffee shop, street corner—wherever—to get it. Or, conversely, you may stay at home and cruise the 'net to get it. Any old which way, you end up doing it often. If this describes you, then you are a slut. And hey—that's okay!

## 2. *Don't Try to Figure Out Why You Are This Way*

Don't psychoanalyze yourself. This is not productive because it's unlikely you'll ever change, at least in this lifetime. Okay, I know the urge to self-psychoanalyze is huge, so I'm going to do it for you. Hopefully, this will purge the urge. If you're gay—especially if you were in the closet for a long time—there may be a reason you're like this. You may have spent a large part of your life being told that you must have romantic love and sex (merged, in some magical way) with a permanent monogamous life partner of the opposite gender. Maybe you tried it, and it didn't work. So you may have, quite naturally, developed an aversion to sex and romance combined. Or, if you had a particularly horrendous family life (and let's face it, who hasn't?), perhaps you find romance and/or affection particularly threatening. Those are two possible reasons you may be a slut. Satisfied? So *please* don't psychoanalyze yourself. And remember, there are a lot of sluts who have had perfectly happy family lives, or were never in the closet at all. You know why they love sex? *Because they love sex.* (It's a tautology, but that's what makes it so wonderful!) Yours is not to reason why, yours is simply to get fucked. Royally. And as often as possible.

## 3. *Don't Listen to What Anyone Tells You about Being This Way*

They may tell you that you are a sex addict. Well, sex is addictive, that's for sure. But you only have a problem (and you will for sure be an unhappy slut) if your work, friendships, and/or romantic life are sabotaged by your sexual escapades. If you can calmly maintain a job and/or friends, and/or a partner and still have sex with a lot of people whenever you want—what's the problem?

People will tell you that you will never find a life partner if you are a slut. Wrong! There are plenty of sluts out there, and though some of them are loners, many of them are looking for partners too. Two sluts are often a perfectly matched set, as long as they're completely honest with each other. (If people tell you sluts never have partners, it's because they're jealous of the fact that you're getting so much sex, and they want to see you suffer.)

People may also tell you that you can be cured of your sluttiness. Well, no. First of all, being a slut is not an illness, and second, you can't be cured.

People will also tell you that you should be ashamed. Why should anyone be ashamed of being a slut? If sex is a good thing (which it is) and healthy for us (if we take the necessary safe-sex precautions) then what's the problem? Only puritans—ashamed, uptight, sad, frustrated people with pinched faces and unfulfilled, icky, pathetic lives—are ashamed of sex. Not you. You're a happy slut!

Finally, people may tell you that all sluts die of AIDS. Not true. You can have as many sexual partners as you want with absolutely no danger—if you don't touch your partners at all. Some sluts, after all, are voyeurs. If you're not primarily a voyeur, then all you have to do to protect yourself from AIDS is recognize that because you have a lot of partners you have to be extra careful about safer sex. What is safer sex? Well, you're an intelligent person! Think for yourself! Read the literature and make your own informed decision.

### 4. Don't Look for Love in All the Wrong Places
This is a common mistake and can turn a happy slut into an unhappy one all too quickly. You can look for sex anywhere you like and anywhere you can find it, but sex is rarely found in the same place love is. The urge, at first, is always to fall in love with the person who gives you the best sex. But this only works in movies and in fantasies. It is rare that two people who are perfect soul mates also happen to be perfect bed mates. So don't look for true love on a gay sex website, or in an alley, or a bathhouse. If you do happen to stumble into a long-term romantic relationship with your very fa-

vorite sexual partner (and this only occurs in rare instances), just remember that good sex usually fades after a few months. Remember not to look for love where you look for sex; you'll just cause yourself pain and anguish. (Don't ask me *why* I know this. I just do.)

5. *Respect Yourself and Others (Even When They Don't Respect You)*
This is probably the most important rule of all. And yet it's the hardest one to obey. It's tough to respect yourself when everybody seems to think that being a slut is a bad thing, and when movies, novels, plays, and your mother all tell you that sluts die alone and unhappy. But you can always respect yourself even if nobody else does—and your own self-respect is a million times more valuable than the respect of others.

Last but not least, respect others even if they don't respect you. Respect the boy (or girl) who's doing crystal meth and passes out in your bed. Respect the guy who seems to hate himself for being gay and fucks you yelling, "Take it, you faggot, take it!" Respect the guy (or gal) you pee on *and* the guy (or gal) who pees on you. Most of all, remember that every consensual sexual act is an act of love. Not an act of being *in* love—an act of love.

The good news is: Because you're a slut, your life will be filled with love. And I promise you, it doesn't get much better than that.

# How to Divine Your Fetish

Suki Lee

*How to Be a Dominatrix*

When looking at your reflection, note that you have the possibility of transformation. You have sought confidence and empowerment, but so far, nothing has catapulted you to the top. You may long to be more articulate, to dispense orders with an acerbic tongue. Your charisma has not yet found its mode of expression, and without an outlet, you remain frustrated. As for your character, you despise being told what to do. You prefer to demand obedience with a dash of order and discipline. You are boundaried. You seek to control the object of your desire. You thrive on taboo.

You go to a fetish party wearing black high-heeled boots. Your breasts are thrust together by a skin-tight corset, untouchable. When people stare at you, choose to look them directly in the eye—or ignore them. Make discriminating choices when searching out a submissive. See bare breasts in front of you. Squeeze the nipples with your gloved fingers. Lick them. Bite them. Smile when she says you bit too hard. She's not the one. Walk on, and find a seat with a good vantage point. Sit with erect posture, and ensure that your flogger's black leather tails are splayed across your fishnets. People will sense your presence in the room. Draw them to you.

Merely looking at you is a painful kind of sexy torture. Note that many subs stare at you as if you are their queen, their omnipotent ruler. They want to give total control over to you. They want you to command them, and lead their flights of fantasy. Choose your sub because her beauty is subversive (the boyish arc of her jaw); choose her because she's the perfect submissive (she gets into a frenzy when your eyes meet). Imagine tickling her with a feather. Imagine blindfolding her. Now, imagine flogging her. Imagine her loving it.

Summon her into your orbit. When she comes to you, she kneels by your side. With eyes lowered, she asks if she can worship your boots. Respond to her directly and with authority. Never answer a question with a question. Speak emphatically, in the imperative, in a tone similar to how I am addressing you now. Your voice is an instrument that can be used to have psychological control over her. She will relish being spoken to in harsh tones. Pull the hair at the back of her head, and tell her she can worship your boots until you get bored. Pull her hair harder for emphasis. That's it. Do you feel that rush? It's the high from giving her pain.

She bends over and takes one of your boots in her hands: such agonizing perfection. She kisses it. She licks it. Her lips trace the bulbous curves of the fat heel as it fills her mouth. While she's sucking it off, your transgression attracts the gaze of onlookers. Gradually, as you start bonding through play, your scene grows into something beautiful. Watch her perform fellatio on your boot. Then disregard her. Finally, dismiss her with a tap of your flogger on her shoulder. Yes, you are understanding how to assert your power.

You may have a streak of exhibitionism. It will prove useful for your next scene. Lead her through the room until you find something to fasten her to. That railing off to the side will do. Excess is permitted—make an opulent display as you bind her to it. With your flogger, spread her legs. Now step back, so you can get a better view of her restrained. She's going to explode unless you start flogging her. Begin now.

The first time you connect the flogger to her, a sudden injection of energy flows up your arm into your body. Surprising, isn't it? It's your experience of pleasure from giving her pain. It will feel exciting and erotic. You will want to hit her again. You may have been vanilla in the past, and part of you may feel like you're crossing boundaries. Unhinge any traditional notions you may still have about sex and socially acceptable conduct. Be conscious of her pain, yet vicious at the same time. Don't fear your cruelty. Give her a good lashing on the backs of her legs, her ass, across her shoulders. Listen to the thud of leather as the flogger's erect tail strikes her. Whip her with increasing savagery. Don't be concerned about it. Just hit her harder (she wants you to). Feel the ecstasy of relief with each impact on her body. Watch her flinch. Bend her like a branch.

Others will take note of your natural talent for domination, circling your star like planets in the universe. The beauty of your sadistic statement will arouse lust. They will want you to dominate them as well.

When it eventually comes to an end, she will be exhausted. As you untie her, the bond between you will loosen. She will thank you profusely. Hold her and make her feel secure as she slowly recovers.

If you ever play with her again, she may ask you to stick her with needles. And if you do, don't feel guilty as you weave them into her thigh. You are in her desire, and you've only just begun.

*How to Be a Submissive*
When looking at your reflection, note that there may be emptiness. I know what it is: your desire is unfulfilled. You want to be humiliated. You want to be objectified. Embarrassment and shame suit your particular psychology. Your experience of eroticism is generated by your powerlessness. You may want someone to lead you, to take the reins and drive you. You enjoy being given orders. Obedience is your forte. You may think your kinks odd, that you're the only one with such fantasies. Take comfort in the fact that you no longer have to watch from the sidelines. Know that you can connect to the next level of understanding, that your body's desire can be liberated through pain.

To attract the attention of a domme, dress scantily in mesh, lace, a collar—anything to show that you are accessible. Your domme stands out. She is a masterpiece in black. Looking at her gives you a rush. You want to submit to her. The mere notion of her dominance over you makes you delirious. Her eyes move through you. You're turned on when she ignores you. Know simply from the way she dresses that she is commanding you. When you see her posing, her hand relaxed on her thigh, you will think about those hands doing things to you: tying you up, gagging you, tickling you, cutting you. When she lets her gaze fall upon you, look at the flogger in her hand and think of it as a bouquet of roses. You will want her to flagellate you with it.

Speak to her and confess your desires. Your eyes will beg her to turn your fantasies into reality. She'll take all the action. In essence, it will be her working for you. And in exchange, you will relinquish your agency. As soon as you start playing, she'll have control over your body—and your mind.

Allow her to collar your delicate larynx until you choke, lightly. Feel that jolt of excitement when she passes her hand across your tit, over your heart, and up to the metal ring in your collar. You get aroused when she ties a leash through the ring, showing her ownership over you. She murmurs that you're her dirty, sweet sub, and you belong to her.

You understand implicitly that she does the talking. All the same, she places a ball gag in your mouth to silence you and fastens the strap around the back of your neck. She whispers in your ear that she's going to bite you, slap you, ride your ass hard. All you can do is grunt in response. The red ball gag is like a small fiery planet stopping up your mouth.

She takes you by the leash and leads you to a spanking bench. You kneel on it with your ass to her. Your heart pounds in anticipation. She teases you with the crop, drawing circles along your back, and moving it across your groin. You hyperventilate when she insinuates it between your legs. Next, she takes the flogger, raises it above you, and lets its leather tendrils cascade gently down your back. Gradually, she uses more force, snapping it forward so its tail stings when it strikes your ass and legs. It sets off a reaction through your body. Each blow makes you tense in pain, then gasp for air. And in that interstice between blows, something like pleasure asserts itself. You are getting all sexed up. You are getting wet. It makes you crave the pain she's giving you. You become anxious to be struck again. You are her muse. Your reaction inspires her. She flogs you more intensely. She marks you like you're a palimpsest, writing over the smooth vellum of your skin. Eventually, you enter a state of delirium, endorphins pumping through your body, setting you alight. The ventricles of your heart open and close. She is speaking to your body in code, in flashes of pain. As you reach the next threshold, the pain turns to ecstasy and then bliss. Euphoric and alive, she brings you to a whole new level. Looking your pain in the eye, looking it in the ass, she knows you're going to come, but she commands you to wait.

This story will end when she wants it to. And you will feel the utmost relief, as one does after being healed. Tonight, you will dream sweetly that she cuts out your bleeding heart and tenderly pricks it with rose thorns. The marks she leaves on your body will be like her arms embracing you tightly, all night long, confined.

# How to Love Your Inner Femme ( … Because We All Have One)

## Mette Bach

The first step to loving your inner femme is finding her, and that might be hard. You might think you've been in touch with her all this time, whenever you paint your nails or curl your eyelashes—or maybe you don't paint your nails or curl your eyelashes, in which case you probably don't think you've been in close contact with her. But even if you look like someone who's in touch with her inner femme, you might still have to coax her out of her shell. Maybe she is hiding behind pain or humiliation, or maybe she is shrouded in abuse or cruelty, or maybe it has been so long since you've even thought about her that she's decided to play hard to get.

All of us are inundated with anti-femme messages: Girlyness and stupidity go hand in hand. Women who pamper themselves are called high-maintenance. Demanding femmes are called divas or princesses. Women who like nice things—and who get them for themselves—are called materialistic. In the straight world, smart women chalk some of these unfortunate realities up to patriarchy. The queer world can't, logically speaking, depend on the same explanation. Maybe that is why each of us should take a minute to look inside and think about our inner femmes. In our world, all genders should be encouraged (it's what we've been fighting for, after all). Each of us has something to learn from our inner femme energy (just like we should all practice accessing our inner butch, queen, and leather daddy).

Many femmes struggle to reconcile their feminist politics with their femme practices. Crises occur in front of bathroom mirrors, in lingerie shops and shoe stores. Even those of us who do not appear very femme—and therefore should not have issues around that particular gender representation—have internalized hurtful messages about what it means to want to wear dresses, to enjoy makeup and miniskirts. Those of us who present girly—to whatever degree—don't necessarily enjoy the assumptions that come with that. We might reject the male gaze. We might be proud of our ability to pitch a tent in stilettos. We might wear combat boots with our corsets. We might throw an unbelievable sucker punch.

I am not an inner-femme whisperer. My own inner femme seems buried and inaccessible most of the time. I think I pissed her off by underestimating her strength. I do not have many suggestions, but I do know that it does not matter what you look like on the outside: Your inner femme can guide you through some pretty exciting and fabulous adventures, if you let her.

Honor her. She is not a cartoon or a stereotype or a caricature. She has nothing to do with that frilly dress your mom made you wear in the second grade for the class photo. Nor was she the reason you succumbed to peer pressure and wore that unflattering glittery number to the school dance. She did not necessarily consent to these things, so do not blame her.

Educate her. She needs skills. She needs to know how to hold a hammer, tie a bowline knot, fix a leaking faucet, speak several languages, and do long division (okay, okay, long division is arguably kind of useless, but she should at least know her multiplication tables). Teach her to cook and grow vegetables because she probably likes self-reliance. Teach her to fix the chain on her bike or change her own tires because she probably likes not having to ask for help. Teach her to invest and save for a rainy day (not just for eyeliner but for stock options, or retirement, or land) because she probably wants to take care of herself. The more skills you give her, the farther she can take you.

Respect her. Feed her properly. Give her eight glasses of water a day and her beauty rest. Let her run and sing and dance and laugh and fall and get up and do it all over again. Let her be free to explore, to find mysteries and wonder, to flirt with danger and to thrive on excitement. Nurture her and she will take care of you right back.

Play with her. Or let her play with you. Let her do your hair. Let her give you a hydrating mask or a pore cleansing treatment. You'll probably like it. Let her take a critical look at your wardrobe and your accessories and your overall appearance. She won't judge you—okay, maybe she will, just a little, but it's for your own good.

Indulge her. Spoil her with a candle-lit bubble bath. If you're new to this, try eucalyptus scented foam bath or gender-neutral juniper. Give her solitude to enjoy her sensuality. Encourage her to want this. Trust her when she asks for these luxuries (because they aren't luxuries; it is necessary to reward ourselves once in a while).

Look at her. I mean really look at her. Get a mirror. Lock your door. Find her. See her. You know what I'm talking about.

Love your inner femme and treat her well, the way you want to be treated.

Queer Wisdom: Our Past, Present, and Future

# An Apology to My Mother

## S. Bear Bergman

Dear Mom,

There are a few things I've been meaning to say for some time now, things that you and I have never discussed, and before it goes any further, I have a few things I would like to apologize to you for.

I'm sorry we never got to giggle about boys. I know you were pretty and popular, and all the boys in the county wanted to take you out when you were a girl, and I know you really were looking forward to talking about dates with me, helping me choose the right top or the right earrings or the right boy for whichever dance, like you got to do.

You would have been good at it, I'm sure, good at all the parts; the talking about boys and sex and curfews, and how to tell if a boy liked me, and all of those key mother-daughter things. But I didn't really *like* boys, and I was too afraid to tell you until it was too late to see whether those skills could have reasonably translated themselves into the world of dating girls, too.

I never told you about my very first date, which I had with a red-headed girl from California who, after that one date with me and one very chaste kiss, went back to her boyfriend in Davis, and, as far as I know, is straight to this day. I never told you about my first time, when I was seventeen, with a beautiful girl on a cold and sunny fall afternoon in her bed at her boarding school, where we spent all day and all night and into the next morning; I never told you that it was better than I could have imagined, languorous and delicious and warm under all of her covers, wrapped up together. I might not have told you if it was with a boy, either, but I think you would have liked to have known, before now, that my first time having sex was safe and honest and everything else you might have hoped for, with a girl I loved very much.

I'm sorry about the shopping. I really am. I know you like it, and I know you had high hopes about long shopping trips for pretty things that we would casually lie about the cost of to Dad, punctuated with little lunches at which we would talk about all kinds of things. I'm sorry shopping was always such an ordeal because I hated everything you liked, and almost all of what I fit into, and we always ended up fighting, one of us crying, until the miraculous method of shopping known as the Lands' End catalog appeared on the scene. But that didn't really offer the same sense of bonding, did it?

When I was eighteen, I thought that going shopping with you to look at girly things was cause for all-out war. Now, nearly thirty, I think, how could it hurt? I don't have to buy it. I wish I had humored you a little in return for all the ways you humored me; I wish I had bent a little bit for as much as you flexed to meet me. The conceits of the young, I guess. But separating seemed so important; I hope you understand I was never trying to reject what you liked by saying it wasn't good or useful, by making it seem silly or by condescending to it. It just wasn't for me. At the time, it seemed so urgent, so vital, to make sure that I shoved femininity away from me as hard as I could, that I protected myself from everything that seemed to come with it, everything I didn't feel comfortable with—and still don't. It took the intervening decade and more to see that, really, I could have just said, no, thank you.

And I'm sorry that now I'm so afraid of what you'll think that I don't take you with me when I go shopping for the things that make me feel good and look good; my peculiar blend of clothes, so masculine but hardly ever manly, with my bright-colored shirts and ties. I wish I felt sure that when I came out of the dressing room, confident and sharp, you'd look at me with pleasure instead of faint shame, that this is your *daughter*, here, in the necktie. But I don't feel sure. So I don't give you the chance.

I'm very sorry about the big wedding. I know what you imagined, the bridesmaids and the shower and the giggling and my great-grandmother's pearl earrings and a lot of people and choosing a wedding dress and shopping for a perfect mother-of-the-bride outfit and picking out china and all of the other business that comes with the wedding process. I keep thinking that maybe we could have made it a little bit more like that, if we'd tried a little harder, instead of the small, perfect, but ultimately frill-free wedding we chose.

All the girl time you didn't get, all the sharing and long brunches and mother-daughter bonding and clashing, all the borrowing of clothes and whatever else is supposed to come with it that you didn't get, I really regret. I feel like my gender cheated you out of something you would have enjoyed enormously, through absolutely no fault of your own.

I know this is late, and there's probably more that I can't think of now. I'm sorry for every time I accused you of not loving me when you were trying to do what you thought was best. I'm sorry I didn't give you better help in understanding what I was doing, and what I was going through, so you could actually judge what might be best. I got afraid of all the parts of it, all the things I thought you couldn't handle or understand, and I decided the best way to keep things civil between us was to hide most of my life and only interact with you on neutral topics. I succeeded in keeping things civil all right, but I prevented us from getting closer, connecting on a deeper level, because I didn't trust you to walk with me where I was going. I can't tell you how sorry I am for that.

I love you very much, Mom. I hope you can accept my apologies and that we can go forward from here, and see what kind of friendship we could have.

Love always—
    S

# An Open Letter to the Newly Bisexual Gay Kid

## Daniel Allen Cox

Dear Newly Bisexual Gay Kid,

Wife divorces sperm donor after bad transaction.

Baby factory closes for renovations.

Breeder with bitch for sale.

These jokes sounded funnier when you were on the other side of the punch line.

There have always been muff-eating fag boys and dykes who love semen. What can you say? People do the things that please them. Sexual outlaws have to deal with a lot of flak, and they spend much of their time resisting the labels that others foist on them. Now your friends can smell foreign genitals on your breath, and they've sicced the bloodhounds on you. They want you to issue a *statement*.

It sucks, you think to yourself, that someone would have to come out twice in one lifetime. It might feel like you're back-pedaling through your accomplishments. There are thoughtful and constructive ways to come out a second time, however, and they don't all involve looking for two hundred new Facebook friends the day after you drop the bomb.

An important adjective to keep in mind is *non-threatening*. Remember that the sexual latencies you have commendably brought to life can be intrusive to your social network (I'm not talking about Facebook anymore). Your queer friends might not be as open-minded as you'd like, and they may have few straight friends of their own. They might be afraid of losing you, forgetting that the bonds of your friendship extend past sex talk and community gossip.

You may even hear whispers of the word *betrayal*, but try not to get too upset. They might be trying to test you, in an infantile way, so be careful to control your reaction. Remember that the real betrayal is being someone you're not.

Confide in your friends that you are actualizing a part of yourself that had been dormant or even ignored. Use language that they have used to describe their own struggle with sexuality. Cobble together words like *discovery* and *shame*, *lust* and *fear*, *acceptance* and *orgasm*, in any order you like, as long as they get the point. Play your favorite mix tapes, the ones that brought you together through summers of beer and pain, rejection and revenge. Pour a wicked cup of tea and touch their hand.

Then, rather than invite them into a straight environment for a first meeting—into enemy territory, as it were—consider inviting your differently sexed partner into your queer milieu. No potlucks, dinner parties, or other events where you suspect the closeness to be uncomfortable. Perhaps a homohop where you can quarter yourself into any number and combination of private conferences, and where you can sneak away for a kiss-and-grope. Your new lover's dance moves might take everyone by surprise, and then you've got nothing to worry about.

Of course, you could always slay them with a stroke of genius and date a differently sexed *queer* person. Queer girls fucking queer boys—anyone challenging that arrangement would be tangled in a slew of parallel ironies. There are too many layers of transgression to possibly criticize. It's just cool.

You have a whole other challenge ahead of you, however, back home in Champaign, Illinois, or Beaconsfield, Quebec, or any other town or suburb that wasn't metropolitan enough for that urbane, queer life of yours.

You have the gloating parents.

Think about it. You fled the small-town nightmare a queer and came riding back a corrected heterosexual. The town might just throw a parade for you: fire trucks shined up; the Kiwanis Club chorus croaking out hymns; and a yellow-brick road of palm branches and spermicidal condoms laid out before your feet.

Your parents, of course, would be the Grand Marshals of the parade. *Congratulations* never sounded so hurtful coming through a megaphone.

These are exaggerations, of course, and that is exactly how it will feel. Your parents may even try their best to avoid humiliating you, but if you've damned them pre-emptively, anything they say will seem like an attack. Trust them not to use your newly explored sexual interests to triumph over you morally. If you treat someone like a criminal, don't they usually commit the crime even if they didn't plan to, just to fit the profile?

Resist the urge to kill the notion, at every opportunity, of you ever having kids. Sure, if Mom hands you knitted booties as soon as you walk in the door, you should probably burn them. If Dad asks you about the wedding, you have every right to ask him about his erectile dysfunction. Many parents are sensitive enough not to ask those questions directly, though most are experts at slanting them into conversation.

If they ask you if you've *changed sides*, praise them for finally being open to discussion. This might be your Trojan horse, your way in past the battle lines. Reaffirm your queerness by not giving them a comfortable label to use. Tell them that you're attracted to different types of people, that you have always felt that way, and that you have a community of friends with similar stories. Kill the grandchildren gently, as it were, and play the adoption card only if you're serious about it.

If you're hardcore enough to bring your new, differently sexed lover home, take your parents out for ribs, and let them see you kiss over a gravy bowl—it would probably be the first time they've let themselves imagine your sex life. A well-timed Ellen DeGeneres-style joke, such as *You kiss even better than a girl/boy*, might help cut the tension. They might even reward your bizarre graciousness by dropping the topic of your sexuality altogether.

How empowering would it be to then mosey into the town's only gay bar on a double date with your parents? They may have always wanted to investigate the seedy hangouts known to their queer child, and you have always wanted to buy a beer there, with enough of a posse not to get beaten up in the parking lot. You will be able to lay claim to the most awesome Facebook status ever:

" ... is recovering from dancing to Le Tigre with Dad and watching Mom do poppers with the bartender."

Of course, that would be an ideal situation. Your own second coming out will probably be more awkward and *why-the-fuck-me?*, but if you take my advice, you will have at least succeeded in escaping the easy labels that people throw around so gratuitously, the ones that make the journey that much harder.

The trick, dear Newly Bisexual Gay Kid, is never to issue a statement.

The trick is to keep them guessing.

Love,
  DAC

# Some Notes to a Young Not-Yet-Femme

## Maggie Crowley

You are seventeen. The day before the big queer youth conference your new vegan, purple, eight-hole Doc Martens come in the mail. You try them on and know that they'll quickly blister your heels, but you can't resist.

You dress in a long, stretchy black skirt and an Oxford shirt from Goodwill. All day you are complimented on your boots and then feel guilty for caring too much about your appearance.

*You will wear that same skirt on a third date with an art student, nervous that she'll think you straight or uncool. You'll lie on your dorm room bunk bed and let her slide her hands up your thighs, pushing the skirt up to your hips. She'll say, "I love skirts" with a sexy foolish grin, and you'll start to understand your body and its power, that you might want to draw someone's gaze to you, that you might be able to draw her gaze and hold it close with your eyes.*

You go to a workshop about labeling, and hear butch and femme explained for the first time. But all you can tell is that femmes wear makeup and dress in feminine clothing. You imagine a white woman dressed in J. Crew separates with blow-dried hair and soft, subtle makeup. She looks like the girls you go to school with or their mothers.

She is not who you want to be. No one talks about being attracted to femmes. No one talks about queering femme, or the distinction between feminine and femme. You sit in a room full of gay boys and young genderqueers and punk hippy girls with shaved heads, and they talk about how they feel restricted by the gender binary. You are appalled at your own selfishness when some small part of you asks over and over, "What about me?"

*It doesn't get any easier to ask for what you need, or to take it. You will bring together women and men like you to talk about fashion and privilege and being seen, to dance, to make cupcakes, to march in the Pride parade. This will always be dangerous ground, because whenever you bring people in, others feel excluded. Over and over again, you claim your space and invite others to claim theirs. It is the best you can do.*

There are so many girls. They have short hair and wear collared shirts or tight white T-shirts or undershirts and baggy jeans. There are a few ties, sometimes worn with women's white blouses, the kind your mother might buy you for a chorus or band concert. Not everyone has figured out how to shop in the men's department.

You talk to some of them, but it's always a results-oriented conversation, about GSAs and safe schools legislation and marriage equality. You don't know how to flirt. You don't know how to approach a stranger without a flyer or a clipboard in your hand.

Your friend Braeden will come out as trans in the next year, before he goes off to Bard, but right now he's a petite butch dyke who goes to the arts academy in New Haven and is sooooo much cooler than you. You're at the big Saturday night dance. Your friends have wandered away, and suddenly you find yourself dancing with him, close, grinding. You keep your knees bent to accommodate his height, hike your skirt up with one hand, the other hand around his waist. You feel a little uncomfortable—you are training him to take over the youth chapter of the marriage equality group, which makes him something like your employee, and he is two years younger, which is a lot in high school. You are dying for him to kiss you and convinced it won't happen.

Since Thursday, when you perched on the arm of his chair and listened in as he outlined a workshop with his friend from Maine, he's been flirting with you and then backing away. He touches your hair or your arm and then starts talking about how hot this or that mutual friend is. All of them are butch or genderqueer or andro. He talks about how marriage isn't the most important issue, which you both agree with and take as a personal rebuke.

On Friday afternoon you come back to check on the marriage equality table, and he pats his lap, asking you to sit. You look at his skinny little frame and hesitate, then awkwardly sit there for a minute, worried that your bony butt is digging into his thighs. Your legs feel gangly and ridiculous, taking up the whole booth, encroaching on the tables on either side.

*You will have slight butch friends and lovers who insist you sit on their laps, and you will keep your feet on the floor and your arm around their shoulders and smile and look down at them and relax your five-feet-seven inches. You will learn the trick of holding your body so that the person you're kissing feels taller, so ze can press hir mouth possessively on yours, even though ze's shorter than you. You will duck your head so you can look up through your bangs at the object of your flirtations. You will wear heels on dates with butches and boys who come up to your armpit. You will wear heels to conferences and protests and fundraisers that you've organized, while riding public transportation and carrying file boxes and cases of bottled water.*

He takes your hand swing-dance style, passes you behind his back, and then spins to his knees, still holding your hand. You smile at him but have no idea what to do. Moments later he's off chasing a baby butch with a pack of cigarettes.

You look around at the goths and the ravers and the hippies and the dykes and feel totally alone. It's not that you want to look like everyone else. It's just that, in a typical piece of high school logic, you are convinced that no one will find you attractive unless you adopt their uniform. That opposites might attract, that your skirts and glitter might intrigue someone, is beyond your wildest dreams.

Late at night in dorm rooms, or at sleepovers in your parents' family room, sharing four sleeping bags between six girls, you talk about sex, or love, you're not sure. The straight girls bemoan their chances of ever meeting a boy. You say you want a girlfriend. Those are the only words you have for your desire.

You don't tell them that on Saturday mornings, putting your hair up in a bun, you imagine that you have a lover who watches you get ready for the dance, who loves the way you look in your leotard and kisses the base of your neck as you expose it, twisting your hair tight and pinning it to your head. You are longing for someone to see who you are and to desire all of it.

Eventually you bring your separate lives together, give up on the endless *Nutcracker* tours and mirrored studios full of straight girls. In a dressing room, which is actually a preschool classroom, you look around at your cast of femmes and assorted other queers and feel for the first time as much at home backstage as you do onstage.

Backstage are three crinolines, shoes, shoes, shoes, fake hair, fake eyelashes, and conversations about sex and touring, and, OMG, tell me about your date. The girl talk is the best part. It's like those long-ago slumber parties but better, because you finally have words for what you want.

# Insider Info for a Foster Nephew

## Wes Hartley

Your teenage hormones are jerking you around by your short-and-curlies. You and all your high school pals are helpless victims. You keep hearing all the guys' bullshit twenty-four/seven about hot-chicks-this and fuckin'-bitches-that. In case you don't know, it's all just show-off big talk and potential-hetero false bravado. It's for sure that all your buddies are whipping it non-stop, same as you are.

You've learned to talk the talk and go along to get along. You're under all this total pressure that never lets up. You conform not because you want to, but because you have to. To survive. Deep inside, you're a freaked-out tangle of confusions and contradictions. You totally can't figure out what the fuck's going on. Or where all these different feelings you're having are coming from.

These certain guys you hang with who you think you know inside out, and who imagine they know all about you (best buds, lifelong pals, bros), don't have a clue—same as you don't. They're all faking it like you are, talking the same bullshit talk and strutting the same wannabe-hetero walk. Not one of them ever hints that he might have doubts about how he feels about girls or about guys, so you don't either. To conform. But deep inside you're freaking out because when you whip it (twenty-four/seven) you're always imagining something hot and dangerous (whatever) with this certain guy. Girls never come into it.

After the pressure's off, you change the subject and the incongruity (what you've always been told you're supposed to be feeling versus the turn-on fantasies driving you to flail your bone) gets put on the back burner. Out of sight, out of mind. It's extra harsh because there's this scary word (a bunch of scary words actually) that you can't hear yourself say deep inside about your secret fantasy world and dangerous feelings. So you keep a lid on it and shove it back down where it won't complicate shit. Shit is way too complicated and fucked up as it is.

Everybody keeps saying there's something definitely wrong and totally not cool about everything queer and faggy and gay. You hear this stated as a fact as though the guys who mouth it off know what they're talking about from firsthand experience. Which they for sure don't! "That's so gay!" is stuff that you never want to be accused of doing or saying or feeling or being. The peer pressure of the gang you run with (and keep in step with) is always cranked up full blast. You and all your buds are constantly under surveillance, monitoring each other, on the alert for any imagined gay infraction. The continual feedback you get on your behavior keeps the tension seriously torqued up. It's not possible to talk about your conflicted feelings to anybody (since I'm not there), so what do you do?

For the time being, don't do anything. By this I mean don't all of a sudden start wondering out loud to somebody if you might be gay because of these different feelings you have about this certain guy. Especially don't say anything to the guy. Keep a lid on everything for a while; start looking for no-bullshit information out there in the big world. Leave your local personal universe just like it is. It's totally fucked up and definitely clueless, but you know your way around in it, and you know better than to fuck everything up by trying to talk about important stuff to guys and relatives who definitely don't have *any* insider info, which is totally the stuff you need to get lots of.

So, where do you start? This book you have in your sweaty hands right now is definitely the kind of place you need to be checking out. There are hundreds more excellent books and articles you need to find. There's the Internet. If you're worried about being spied on by somebody at home or at school, then go to a computer at a public library or to one of those dollar-an-hour Internet cafés.

The fact is that there are millions of guys of all ages who have the same feelings for guys that you have. I'm serious. Everything you feel deep inside is one hundred percent totally normal and natural. And good. You've been brainwashed by society and by peer pressure to believe that there is something wrong or uncool or not masculine about the way you feel.

Freeing yourself of the brainwashing is called deprogramming. It's totally possible to deprogram yourself, but it's way better and easier in the long run to find some other young guys who have gone through what you are going through. These are the guys who can answer most of your important hard questions and protect your sensitive feelings while you're figuring everything out. They can help you delete all the heavy-duty programming from your negative hard-wiring.

All I can tell you for sure is that you *will* get it all figured out. You *will* finally learn that your feelings are perfectly normal and natural and manly, and you *will* meet lots of other guys who have the same feelings you have. I guarantee this.

From here on everything gets a whole lot better in many ways, the important one being finding lots of guys like yourself who you can open up to, who will totally back you up, be on your side, show you a thing or two. The "thing or two" I'm referring to will definitely be worth checking into seriously when the time comes, and you *will*, trust me.

For now, be cool and stay focused. Soon your confused feelings will sort themselves out, and you'll start meeting guys outside your neighborhood gang and school who will have seriously personal stuff in common with you. I guarantee it. These new allies, new buds and total bros, will share their insights and experiences; eventually, at your own speed and when the time is right, you'll be able to share your inner life with any of your long-time pals and family that you are comfortable with.

You *can* accomplish this. If you've ever done research for a school theme paper or totally checked into some subject you got interested in, you'll know how to get going. If you've never done this kind of detective work, it's time you did.

Take it slow and easy. Pay attention to all the signals and warnings. They are all there for good reasons. Try to be positive and optimistic. Keep remembering that you're *not* alone in this, and that you will soon be hooking up with all kinds of other guys with whom you can share your experiences and feelings.

I advise you to look for guys your own age or maybe a year or two older, at the most. For now. Way older and way more experienced guys are okay to mentor you and *talk* with you about their experiences, but that's it. Don't permit them to sweet-talk you into doing anything physical. If any way-older guy starts to get too personal or touchy-feely, whatever, hit the road immediately and slam the fuckin' door behind you. Make it your rule to keep the touchy-feely stuff special between you and young guys your own age who you might have certain personal feelings for. Okay? It'll be way better this way, and you and your buds will be able to figure out different stuff at your own pace and in your own natural way.

I've suggested that you go outside of your familiar gang of buds and your school to find young guys like yourself, so that you can keep everything in your local routine going along as usual for the time being. In large cities there are support groups for guys (and girls) your age with drop-ins and safe zones, where you can socialize and talk about stuff and hook up afternoons after school and on weekends. Find out if there is such a place where you live, and definitely check into it. These groups are mentored by responsible, sympathetic, seriously righteous people (like your good old uncle) who are totally on your side and will help you however they can. In no time, you'll be hooked up with new pals and (who knows) somebody special ...

You *can* do this. I promise you, it gets way better and way easier. Your good old uncle knows the territory because he's been there, done that. He just wants to smooth the path for his favorite nephew all the way up that sunshiny yellow brick road and back safe and sound to Kansas, or wherever. Okay?

# To My Thirteen-Year-Old Daughter, Who Just Told Me She's Bi

Sean Michael Law

We sat at the dining room table, you (with your new black hair) and Matt and me, and talked about coming out. How it felt, what it meant, how it *would* feel sometime later for you. And I said to Matt, "She really doesn't want to listen to two old gay men talking about what it's like to be queer." I knew it was true. Your grin—out from under your long hair and that cap pulled low onto your forehead—confirmed it. I still know it's true as I write you this letter.

Even so, I can't tell you what I'm going to type because I've never written a letter like this. But I can tell you one thing: I will find words to say. Not knowing what's coming next is maybe the most surprising thing about being queer in the world. Improvisation has, time and again, led to confidence.

Let me start with a story.

When I grew up, I wanted to play piano. I wanted it more than I wanted most things (aside from wanting to be a paleontologist, which pretty much steamrollered any other desire). I was in the sixth grade when my mother (your grandma) bought me an upright piano. It was like one of those old pianos you'd see in a saloon—brown wood and boxy, but with a shine that begged to be touched. I was thrilled. Thing was, Mom could only afford the piano and not lessons.

I didn't care. Every day when I came home from school, I'd tinker on the piano. I learned the difference between the white keys and the black keys. I learned how to play scales. I learned rudimentary, familiar tunes like "Greensleeves" and the riff from Beethoven's

Ninth Symphony. My mother told me that my grandfather (your great-grandfather) learned on his own, and so probably I could too.

As you know, I'm no master pianist these days. But I learned something by trying it on my own—that without the structure of lessons, without the intention of daily practice, I still managed to feel close to my piano and to make music on it without being intimidated. And I learned to appreciate the way all those keys worked together. I learned to improvise, and to be confident in my improvisations.

Which is like writing this letter to you. And which is like being queer.

You know I have no advice for you. Being queer is like being an artist—it's different for everyone. But if I had to give you advice, or encouragement, it would be as simple as two words: be fearless. In fearlessness you will find your footing, and you will uncover what is so wonderful about being queer.

No one can tell you what you are. You don't need anyone to tell you. You've decided what is true about yourself, what is crystal clear and exuberant, a realization that has made you impervious. It's as though you sat down at a piano and plucked out a tune that sounded the same as your thoughts. And no one else can claim to know that melody. Everyone else is just audience. You can sit back confidently, knowing you've claimed the space around you for yourself.

Confidence alone won't help you be fearless, though. Confidence is only one ingredient.

See, being queer isn't about being just one thing. It's about understanding the harmony of all things, the necessity of difference and the careful ways that human lives integrate with one another.

But let me put it another way.

Let's go back to the piano. The thing about pianos is that their very separate keys come together to create unified sound. Potential discord can become harmony. But in order for that to happen, the pianist must understand how keys play together.

For most beginners, the piano is all about the white keys. They're easier to play; they're not as challenging as those little odd-sounding black keys. But no piano music is complete without black keys, without flats and sharps. You may be able to pluck out a tune on white keys alone. But you won't be able to make *music* without involving all the keys. When a musician understands that it takes all the notes to make a song, then he can be fearless in his improvisations and inventions.

You can be fearless because you know something special now. You know about the harmony between black and white keys, between male and female, and between queer and straight. A lot of straight, gay, lesbian, bisexual, and transgendered people might want you to believe that there is a firm line between being queer and being not-queer. They will want you on their side; they will want to be able to count you among their numbers. The most generous, sweet, kind, loving people may nonetheless demand that you agree with them. It's not unlike the peer pressure and harassment you've lived through in middle school. It's unsettling, and it can ruin more than your day.

But there's a secret that you already know that makes you impervious. You have a straight mother, a gay father (and stepfather), a Spanish grandma, and a German grandma. You have an aunt who is Muslim and friends who fit only into their own scene. You know all there is to know already about being queer, and that's the knowledge of harmony. Of all things working together to make music.

A queer life is a lyrical life. None of us, queer or not-queer, ever stops performing or listening to other people perform. But where some people hear dissonance or competition, where others will not listen to other people singing, won't hear what they have to say, the queer performer hears all the parts of the symphony.

So be confident when you compose your song. There will never be a circumstance that won't need your song to play. And listen to those playing around you. There will never be a circumstance where their songs are not needed, too.

Welcome to the lyrical world.

Love,
Dad

# Letter to a New Generation of Gate Keepers

Lloyd Meeker

I'm writing this letter to you in the fervent hope that you will come to believe something. If you don't believe it now because it seems too crazy or impractical, I ask that you put the idea aside gently, making room for the possibility of believing it at some time in the future. This idea is the single most important thing that I can give you. When you do believe it, you will see with new eyes and new heart as the world offers unexpected possibilities to you—possibilities invisible to most.

You have been given a great and sacred gift—you are gay. Some peoples called us "Two-Spirited," and held an honorable place for us in daily life. You might be surprised how many cultures viewed men like us with respect. That, as you well know, has not been the historical experience in mainstream North American culture.

I want you to believe that your being gay is not a meaningless fluke. You are gay for a reason—the Universe has entrusted you with stewardship of a certain kind of spiritual consciousness and power that no heterosexual man can ever carry. It is entrusted only to people like us.

I'm not saying this to make you feel grandiose. I'm saying this because you have important work to do. This work is found on a spiritual path that is open only to men like us, and traveled by comparatively few of those to whom the path is open at all.

When I say a spiritual path, I want to make sure you understand the distinction I draw between religion and spirituality. Religion is a formal system of doctrine, behaviors, and belief that offers to codify our relationship to universal spirit. I see spirituality as the evolving, unstructured, and direct individual experience of universal spirit.

For some, the highly defined paths of religion provide an adequate spiritual experience. I don't think there's anything wrong with that. But for others—and I think you are one of them—the inner guidance of the soul leads away from and beyond the comfortable certainty of those conventional structures. That begins a much more demanding journey, but its rewards are unspeakably beautiful and full of creative power.

The spiritual path for many of my generation focused on awakening—realizing that in spite of being taught that homosexuals were broken, disgusting, or pathetic, we were spiritually and morally right to be ourselves. We lucky ones then learned to live openly, insisting that we be given the same societal and legal rights that heterosexuals enjoyed. I think it's fair to acknowledge that this spiritual awakening among us was resisted and condemned most vehemently by followers of religions who did not see our openness as a spiritual awakening at all, but the work of their devil. Although many of those religious folk might not agree, that battle is over. Spiritual awakening won.

Now a bigger job lies ahead precisely because that awakening occurred, and I think the job belongs mostly to you and your generation. What is homosexuality *for,* in spiritual terms? What does it mean to be a spiritually alive gay man bringing his unique gift into the world?

A beginning point in understanding the sacred gift of homosexuality is self-evident: you are different from the majority of human beings. Regardless of what ethnic or cultural minority a gay man might belong to, he is still a minority within that. I believe we are supposed to be a minority.

The core of our gift is the energy of the Other—so similar, yet mysteriously different. Being different doesn't mean better than others, but it certainly doesn't mean less than, either. In our generation, some sought to establish an in-your-face defiance to honor our difference. Others wanted to get married and raise children in the suburbs, complete with dogs and a station wagon. While I don't think either of those interpretations of our spiritual awakening is wrong, I also don't think they are adequate models to guide your generation in expressing the beauty and power homosexuals can bring to society.

Bear in mind that our generation had very few who modeled for us what being openly, authentically, and triumphantly gay would look like. While we had many wonderful inspirational elders like Leonardo da Vinci and Walt Whitman to look to, we had almost no social mentors. We had to be our own cultural midwives. Defiance and assimilation were two of our most important experiments.

Some will suggest that you really are just like a heterosexual except for the incidental fact that you love your own gender. I disagree. I tell you that the reverse is wonderfully, shockingly true: you happen to love men because you are wired so differently than heterosexuals. I don't think gay men should be concerned about assimilation or difference any more. There is no more need to be either artificially different or artificially similar to heterosexuals. Finding out what it means to be naturally, authentically both similar and different will lead you to spiritual power.

When I was coming out, I was fascinated to read that the Dagara people in West Africa call homosexual men Gate Keepers. In their way of seeing, Gate Keepers are responsible for maintaining the living connection between the earth and the spirit world. If this living connection between the invisible and the earth is lost, the earth will die. What an interesting vision—that the very survival of the earth depends on homosexuals!

What if this spiritual role of Gate Keeper were true not just metaphorically but literally? What if the job of every gay man was to keep certain energies alive in the earth, without which the earth would perish? I am absolutely convinced it is so.

How can you find out what—if any—of this is true for you? When I finally accepted that I was gay, I was a minister in my mid-forties, married, with a family. Since then my journey as a gay man—including divorcing, declaring bankruptcy, changing careers, getting sober, building a new life, surviving a pulmonary embolism, needing surgeries for cancer, and marrying a wonderful man—has required one thing of me: to listen to what originates from the other side of the particular Gate I keep. Any advice that I have for you is based on what I've learned by that listening.

Listening is a challenging and inexact discipline. It took courage for me to listen. What I heard through my Gate was so different from what I heard around me, often different even from my own internal voices. Learning to listen like this takes practice. As you practice, you will discover astonishing things about yourself and the world you live in. I suggest you try doing something gentle to raise your receptivity while you are listening. Meditation, writing, and music have been important for me. Tai chi, gardening, or working with animals could be just as effective, I think.

To listen well, I think you must cultivate a sense of wonder. The clever, bitchy ennui that has been fashionable among men like us serves no purpose in Gate Keeping that I can see. At the risk of seeming naïve, celebrate your happiness in small things—it's great exercise for the spiritual ear. Being delighted to see things anew and to be amazed by the familiar will improve your ability to listen. Be open to noticing little surprises at the periphery of your perception and imagination. Not every such surprise will be a message from the spirit world seeking your attention, but some might be the envelope, so to speak, containing a message.

Practice kindness and friendship, hallmarks of spiritual strength. I can't emphasize this enough, so I won't try. Gate Keeping is a discipline of the heart, and through the heart you will find your tribe of like-hearted souls—straight and queer, all together.

This work will change you and, through you, the world around you. Whether those changes seem small or big to you, they will be profound. There's much more to Gate Keeping than I've put in this letter, but I expect this is plenty for now. Think of Gate Keeping as a performance work-in-progress rather than a static, well-defined job. Given the chance to exercise, your spiritual gifts will grow and evolve with age. Learning to share those gifts with the rest of the world is a lifelong project from which there is no retirement. We lucky ones, we grow old and get more time to practice, more time to feel the fulfillment of being a Gate Keeper. May you be lucky, too.

You have a wonder-full path of pioneering ahead of you. You are a young man of remarkable quality and gifts. If there is anything I can do to assist you, to encourage you, to support your growth, I'd consider it an honor to help as I can. After all, my fulfillment as a Gate Keeper requires that I assist your generation in carrying our spiritual gift in ways that mine could not. But you will have to ask me for my input—otherwise I may offer more advice than you want!

I am certain that you and your fellow Gate Keepers will become more adept than we in my generation have been. Then you will help the generation after you in the same way. Only through this continuity will we ensure that the particular Gates between the visible and invisible for which gay men are responsible are sustained, that they flourish. I don't know how you will do your part, but I am certain you will keep your Gate beautifully. Blessings in profusion to you on your journey.

# Advice for My Younger Self

## Andy Quan

You are different. This is fine, good even. Everyone is different, from each other, from the crowds around them, but many don't know that.

They think that difference is bad, as you are discovering. A part of you knows already that they are wrong. Trust that part.

Hesitate less. Speak up more. You have many valuable things to say, even at a young age. People may not listen. But they might.

Time really does pass more quickly as you age. It may not feel like that now as you are lying in our TV room watching dust float in the air, set alight by the sun. How will you ever get out of this place? But you will. You will find your way.

For many years, how people see you in relation to the shape of your eyes, the color of your skin, will be primary to your life. This is not all bad. You will learn much from it. The complexities of our prejudices. Resilience. Community. All of us come from somewhere. All of us are unique.

It will confuse and confound you to face racism within your own chosen community. But I tell you, it will one day be less important. The world will change for the better.

Fantasize less. Get out more. Go on a few messy dates. That second boy, the one you meet after the first one hurt you, kiss him as long as you can. Let him go all the way. Don't hold back or be afraid. It won't last long, but it could be sweet, and when you see him—after a year away, walking with the new red-haired girlfriend he'll later marry and with whom he'll have a child—you won't regret the way that you curled into yourself as if around a stone, away from him. As if there was time to unfold.

You will trust in astrologers and clairvoyants because they can see into the future, and they will show that you will live. You will not die at a young age. Just because you cannot picture yourself being older does not mean that you will not get there. But trust less in soothsayers. They will be right about half of the time, but you will spend far too much time pondering the other half.

It's right to gravitate towards cities and communities that are diverse. Life is too short to spend it fighting, to spend it not being accepted. You're excited by creativity and commerce and the cogs that make society turn, by ideas and architecture. There will be benefits from living in small towns but you'll feel trapped, you won't feel alive until you're out of there; you won't find your posse, your kin.

Desperation is not particularly pretty. Try to want less. Lovers will come when you are not hoping for so much or working so hard.

You will be an activist. It is a positive thing to care deeply about something and to fight for it. You will learn organizing skills, patience, adaptability, and tenaciousness. Use anger to motivate you, but don't stay angry too long. Try to spend little time with those who are angry all the time; they will drain you. Think compassionate thoughts as you are speeding away.

About that man who looks into your eyes and holds your glance—stop thinking with your head. Feel him somewhere below. It doesn't matter if you don't know if he's gay or not. Or if he's hinted about a girlfriend. Or if you think he has a boyfriend or he's implied that himself. He can make a choice, as you can. Why is it of importance that he's flying out in a day, that he doesn't live in the same city? This is not for life. And, in fact, it never will be. Even if it is, you'll need to go in, day-by-day, live in the present, be in the now, all that jargon that you'll come to know. You can be romantic without being fantastical. You can have ideals without being unrealistic.

And why not kiss a frog, or a bear, an otter, a pup or a lion? A bit of experience won't hurt you. Who are you waiting for? Seriously.

You will meet him aged twenty-one. And another when you're thirty-two. And one at thirty-seven. So before, and in-between, and after each: Fool around. Get messy. Fumble. Kiss. Grope. Shag. Focus on the things you like, and if things aren't working out, try to be kind and respectful and clear and final.

Exercise more. You aren't as unathletic and uncoordinated as you thought. You're prone to depression, and exercise will help your moods. It will also help you meet men in the clubs or the streets. It's attractive to be fit. Sometimes you will think you are unhappy, but you really just need to be more active.

You will confuse loneliness for other problems in your life. During your first difficult job, you will daydream about a perfect man. You will think an embrace will solve culture shock. You will eat poorly, feel tired, and want the food of love to give you energy. You will lack friends or be far from the ones you have: *love, love, love,* your mind will repeat—though it's not necessarily what you'll need.

Be cautious about drugs. It's a good idea not to jump in too early. The brain is still developing all the way to adulthood. Why fuck that up? A little experimentation, sure. Maybe wait until your late twenties, even thirties? There's time.

You will find yourself, sometimes, in the wrong time and place, where you are unappreciated, unattractive, dateless, desperate, and alone. The truth: There is nothing wrong with you. You will do as much as you can to improve the situation (I applaud this). But you just need to move. Or wait.

Conceit and vanity are unattractive, but you're far from those dangers. Appreciate the wonders of your young body, the way it heals quickly, your full head of hair, your slim waist. It's not that you'll miss these things: looks become less important. But while you have them, celebrate. Do a little jig. In the mirror, see fewer faults and more beauty.

Some of what I am telling you, you know already. Other parts of the future will remain mysterious.

One day you will wish you could have traveled back in time to give a bit of guidance to your younger self making his way through this confusing gay world. Perhaps to say:

*You will fall in love. He will be as kind as you ever dreamed.*

# Letter to a Young Man in Early Winter
# from a Train, or How to Love

## Michael Rowe

December 12, 2007

Dear B.,

I'd forgotten how immaculate the countryside outside Ottawa looks after forty-eight hours of snow, and I am struck by it as the train takes me back home to Toronto this afternoon. The way the rolling hills plane out across farmland and sloping dells mantled in an ermine blanket of white, but with trees winter-flowered from tip to base, takes me back across the decades. I had forgotten the degree to which southern Ontario, where I now live, is so much less dramatic than the rocky, hilly landscape of eastern Ontario outside our mutual hometown. It all comes back to me now in a hibernal wash of brilliance through the windows of the train. The spiky, leaf-less trees against the background of ice-blue sky, the hills, the frozen marshes, they all rush past like steam.

Even now, having settled far from here and having made a life with one special man I'm legally allowed to call "my husband," I can't forget that Ottawa is the town in which I was born. I "own" this jagged, granite landscape in a strange sort of way, or at least it owns me. Did I tell you on the train that one of the things I love best about you is how much you love this landscape too? It was our first kinship, wasn't it? Shared roots in this special part of the world.

B., I miss you already and wish you were on the train with me, but you've chosen to stay in Ottawa for a few more days to spend some time with your friends and your family. At my reading and book-signing this summer, I admit to having been delighted and flattered to meet such a handsome young reader. Later, when I found out who you were, and how extraordinary your life accomplishments already are, literary and otherwise, I had to revise my initial impression slightly, but only to enhance and burnish it as I realized I could learn as much from you—still in your early twenties—as you might learn from me. This is a sobering thought as I move into mid-life, but not an unpleasant one.

I'm glad you made this trip to Ottawa with me. It's been fifteen years since I was there, and it's a haunted city. How much more fulfilling to revisit it with you. I feel like Scrooge, hand in hand with a happy young spirit taking me into my own past. I spent so many of those years aching and removed from any sense of roots: the nascent early-1970s gay boy with the foreign service parents and only the most tenuous sense of a home address, let alone a hometown; a sissy, already alien to the world of normal boys no matter where in the world we lived, alien even to myself in those pre-*Ellen*, pre-high school, "gay/straight alliance" days (days you take for granted now).

When did my generation become the "point generation," the generation with as many years behind us as in front of us? When did we become the generation that looked in the mirror one day and suddenly saw the reason why we were being called "sir" by young men and women we'd thought of (in the abstract at least) as the same age as us, or having guys wolfishly size us up as "older men" or (God help us) "daddies"?

What conclusions do people come to when they see you and I together? Does it depend on the situation? The locale? Do they see a father and son? An older boyfriend and his younger partner? Mentor and protégé? Teacher and student? Friends? Or do we not register at all?

How do I feel about that? How do *you* feel about that? Do either of us have any control over it? Does it even matter? Ultimately, of course, it doesn't. We're building our own history as friends in the *now*, and only you and I will truly know what elements comprise that friendship. Our meeting last summer is already part of a past we're making up as we go along.

But it does lead to some interesting questions about the nature of what's real, in gay life, and what is just another of the stunning illusions we seem to craft better than anyone else. Like the brilliant landscape outside the windows of the train, subtly shaped and altered by snow, by the leafless winter snap of blue and white that will look so different in six months. Same landscape, just ... *different*, depending on when you see it. Or who you are when you look.

All we can do is record it, and try to remember who we were when it happened.

I wish you'd met my friend E. at the station the night before last, when we arrived, but your mother met our train and picked you up, and E. couldn't meet the train. I took a taxi to his house instead.

You'd like him, I think. He's very easy on the eyes in a Mountain Equipment Co-op way, rugged, solid, and manly in the forest ranger style. I've always thought of him as being the archetypal hot camp counselor you'd have a blinding crush on over the course of one magical, humid summer you'd still remember when you were an old man.

Mostly, though, E. is one of the kindest men I've ever known. I was smitten when we met and remain smitten today. I think the current pop-culture term of your generation is "bro-mance," with or without the hyphen.

I hadn't seen E. for nearly a year. When he left Toronto to move home to Ottawa, it was like a piece of me was severed. Some friendships are so vital—in the sense of being alive—that their absence creates an emotional "phantom limb" syndrome. E. and I would meet at the park near my house in Toronto to walk our dogs for an hour or so at twilight, down by the ravines near the Don River. It was just him and me, plus my two Labs and his Nova Scotia Duck-Tolling Retriever. We walked every evening, in every season, for more than five years, in rain, shine, snow, fog, and anything else. I remember the comforting sight of his shoulders in his nylon foul-weather gear when he walked ahead of me. I remember his smile and the way he made me laugh when he spoke in the dogs' voices, expressing what we suspected were their true thoughts about us.

For five years, we talked about everything. I vetted his girlfriends for him whether he welcomed it or not. When I did a thumbs-down, even if he resented it, I was usually right.

I told him things I'd never told anyone else about myself. We became part of each other's private histories. We hold those five-plus years in each other's hands. I love him in a wonderfully instinctive, uncomplicated way, and I have every reason to believe it's reciprocal. Then, suddenly, one day it sank in that he was somewhere else, and that moment of time was gone forever, but we have the history and the memories we made.

But back to the present. Remember how I prayed for snow in Ottawa while I was there? I told you I wanted snow, just like when I was a kid.

I wanted to try to see with those eyes, to see where I'd come from, and where I'm going now. The snow began to fall the night I arrived, and it continued unabated for the next day and night, canceling definite borders, blurring lines, creating veil upon veil, worlds within worlds.

After dinner last night at one of the chic bistros that seem to be making Ottawa hip in spite of its patrician, if slightly dowdy mien, E. drove me back to my old neighborhood.

At ten o'clock, it was dead quiet. There was no wind, just silence, and the snow fell down like a white wall in the blackness. With the Christmas lights on the snow banks and the dark houses set back from the road, it looked like we had stepped back in time. And suddenly, there I was on our street. Our family's house looked the same—maybe a bit smaller to me now, but not significantly. I looked at a tree in front of the house and tried to picture myself small enough to have climbed it. I tried to remember a time when the earth was still sufficiently cold to produce enough snow that my brother and I were able to leap off the roof of the house and fall into the back yard, buried up to our necks.

E. and I took a meandering walk down streets I knew so well as a boy. Not much had changed. The water tower had been dismantled, and a new housing complex had been built in its stead, and the firehouse had been updated and modernized.

But still, by God, it was the 1970s somewhere on those streets, and I expected to meet myself, tall and thin and young, walking quickly down the snowy streets, all wrapped up in a scarf and a hat. Sixteen years old, maybe, dreaming of love or fame or both, daring to believe that either was possible, yet filled with a horrible dark dread—cold as the winter itself—that the imminent owning of my true self, my true desires, would bring my entire world crashing to a halt, or end my life, or something equally portentous. No wonder I lived in my head so much. It was a much lovelier and more optimistic place.

But last night with E. was like walking through a dream. Everything—the snow, the Christmas lights, even E.'s strong, handsome presence, a stand-in for the ghosts of so many of the teenage guys I walked with in the '70s, halfway in love—was in hyper-focus, as though time had turned in on itself in a Möbius strip where the past and the present met. Behind the dark windows of sleeping houses, my memories flitted and played. At one point I reflexively leaned over and touched a snow bank just to make sure that it was real.

That *I* was real. It was like waiting for my own adolescent ghost to come rushing out of the winter darkness towards me.

I would have liked that. I would have liked to sweep that boy up and hold him close and let him know it was all going to work out fine, that he would love and be loved.

I would have liked to tell him that loving is so much easier than hating, that there are several roads that lead away from the brutality of childhood taunts and early lessons in bigotry and the hate of difference, and that not all of them lead to bitterness. Some lead to a place of strength and acceptance of ourselves and the world, an awareness that we have the power to change it, to protect others who can't protect themselves. To live a fulfilled, dignified life with courage and grace. To be generous and fearless in love, and forgiving in our fury. To understand that anger and rage are not the same thing—that the first is impotent and confusing, while the second can be the fuel to make the world a better place. That the real lesson in liberation is the ability to be kind: to ourselves, to each other in our immediate community of brothers and sisters, and then to the wider world. To someday learn to nurture and care for the next generation without exploiting it, without demanding anything from it other than letting it enjoy its own moment of youth and beauty and discovery. To embrace and become the totality of our experiences, and all the people we've loved, even long after they're gone.

I could tell you all those things, B., but I sense you already know them, or are at least starting to. You don't need life lessons from me. You have accomplished more in twenty-three years than some men accomplish in an entire lifetime. *I* could learn from *you*, if you'll let me. The ghost in the snow isn't you, it's me. I am my own history, as you will someday be yours. It's beautiful, believe me.

All my love,
 Michael

Practically Queer

# Hopes, Dreams, and a Little Marriage Advice

## Dr Kevin Alderson

In 2003, as I was getting pumped to write a different manuscript, an editor at Insomniac Press asked me to co-author a book with Dr Kathleen Lahey about same-sex marriage. Over the next few months, I interviewed forty-three individuals, representing twenty-two married or soon-to-be-married couples living on three continents. The following year, *Same-Sex Marriage: The Personal and the Political* hit bookstores, and by then, a new domino effect was spreading: same-sex marriage was becoming legalized in several Canadian jurisdictions.

In my interviews with these people, many of whom were among the crusaders who fought for same-sex marriage in Canada, I asked them to share their advice for those who may be getting married. Here is what I learned, and what you can, too.

*Their Hopes and Dreams for You*
It took a lot of soul searching for you to finally come out as queer, but at some point along the path to finding yourself, you discovered that your attractions or your identity did not jibe with the heterosexual majority. With that discovery came the incredible gift of giving voice to feelings of being different. You were raised in a homophobic society, however, and you internalized our culture's mores and values. You possibly struggled with overcoming internalized homophobia, fear, anger, guilt, shame, and/or self-doubt, which may have contributed to deep feelings of self-loathing. Some of you came to seriously contemplate or attempt suicide. The path toward self-acceptance has not been easy because you are constantly reminded of the continuing defamation of character that has systematically been

launched against queer individuals. Some people in society hate you without knowing you, while others turn a blind eye to that which they don't understand. Either way, you grew up in a world that denigrated you, whether because of your love for someone of the same gender, or because your true identity conflicted in some way with what was expected of you.

You may have been reminded of your inferior status—in the minds of many—when you became proud enough of yourself that you began to disclose your identity to others. Your desire to be honest and your hope of garnering some support may have been challenged. How can anyone describe the anguish that results when people you are close to are shocked or horrified by your queerness?

Sometimes you felt alone in a jungle of hostility. Although it is common to see heterosexual couples kiss or walk hand-in-hand in public, you may have felt too afraid of other people's reactions to do the same. It's not about flaunting your sexuality, but when you care deeply about someone, some physical contact seems natural. However, your natural tendency to show affection may have been betrayed by fear of repercussion. You know all too well that abuse toward queer people, whether it is verbal or physical, remains prevalent.

We look forward to the day when you can be yourself wherever you are. You should feel safe as you walk down the street without fear of reprisal. Prejudice and discrimination should be a thing of the past, but it is not.

If you are living in Canada, remember that the Charter of Rights and Freedoms has been a tremendous gift, but changes still need to happen in society. You have a right to insist that schools be safe for everyone, not just those who belong to the majority culture. School personnel need to be better informed about you. Their occupation is education, yet many do not understand that you too are worthy of dignity and respect instead of fear, hatred, or ostracism.

You need to stop hating parts of yourself, and that will only happen as you continue working on overcoming your internalized homophobia. Societal changes are occurring, but as they unfold, focus on maximizing your potential and do not settle for second best in life. You were born equal to everyone else, and you will die that way as well.

Accept and love others in the queer community. Nurture each other—our queer family has been divided long enough. Stop creating and living by hierarchies of what you might think is acceptable for other queer individuals. Gay men, lesbians, drag queens, leathermen, bisexuals, transgendered, transsexuals, and others who avoid labels all comprise our community, and each has their place. Be who you are and let others do the same.

Don't equate love and sex. Sex is not everything, and marriage is a testament to that truth. Marriage is no longer an institution exclusively for heterosexuals, and there is a lesson for all of us in the inclusiveness of this societal gift. You do not need to see marriage through the eyes of patriarchy, for example. Relationships can be constructed in many ways, each of which can be egalitarian.

The legalization of same-sex marriage is not the end of fighting for queer rights—discrimination and homophobia remain rampant. We encourage you to continue the struggle for equality, liberty, and justice for all. Your voice must be strongly heard.

*Marriage Advice: Think About It Before You Do It*
Carefully consider marriage before embarking on it. Don't do it on impulse. Overall, consider longer courtships rather than shorter ones. As you mature, your relationship will mature as well. Life experience is necessary for any relationship to thrive. You need to have a strong self-identity in order to commit to another person.

Don't marry simply because you have the right to do it now; don't marry for political reasons. Wait until your partner already feels like your family. You need to have confidence in yourself and in your partner. Live together first and see how that fits for you.

Ask yourself, "Is this the person I can be myself with for the rest of my life?" Be honest with yourself, and be honest with your partner. Remember that being yourself isn't as difficult as being who you are not.

### Relationship Advice: Love is the Foundation
Understand, before you marry, that living common-law and getting married have different legal ramifications, depending on where you live. Do the research to find out these differences. Realize that by getting married, you are not only taking on something for your community, but you are taking on some of the homophobia as well. Same-sex marriage is making a public statement about your relationship to your partner.

Build a strong foundation for your relationship. You'll need these four cornerstones for a good marriage: 1) being attuned to each other, 2) being supportive of one another, 3) loving each other, and 4) being able to express yourself sexually with one another.

Before you marry, make sure you and your partner are compatible, and on the same page. Discuss issues such as money, family traditions, children, life goals, and so forth—before you commit. While you need common goals and interests, also appreciate that it is the differences that make for an interesting life together.

Know that intimacy does not end in the bedroom. It is an expression of tenderness toward your partner throughout daily living. Loyalty and fidelity are important in a marriage. That doesn't necessarily mean monogamy is the only option, but whatever lifestyle you choose, make sure you and your partner have discussed and agreed upon it. Resiliency is a characteristic of a hearty relationship. Your relationship will have many ups and downs, and you simply can't crack apart at the seams every time life hands you misfortune, conflict, or disease. Your partner should be your best friend.

Romance remains important in a good relationship. When you catch yourself taking your partner for granted, shake things up again by doing something romantic. Don't let your spark, or your partner's, wither away under the mundanities of everyday living. Kick it up a notch every now and then.

Treat your partner with respect and dignity. Provide him or her with encouragement, support, praise, and critical feedback when necessary. Your partner, who soon will become your spouse, deserves the very best from you.

An important part of commitment is freedom of expression. You need to give each other space. Your goal is not to change your partner—instead, accept the good and the bad in him or her. It's not easy, but you need to appreciate and accept both the positive and the negative attributes of your partner. Perfection has no place when dealing with human beings who are trying to be honest and sincere with you.

Relationships are hard work and perseverance is one of the keys to a good relationship. Marriage won't cure your problems, so deal with them. Relationships involve constant work and effort: they are both wonderful and difficult. If you need help to improve your relationship, get it.

The roles you assume in your relationship depend upon the needs, strengths, and weaknesses of each of you. Strive for equality. We can invent our own traditions for same-sex marriage. At present, we have no role models to follow, but you can be each other's role model.

Communication skills are the most important key to a good relationship. Don't just communicate the easy stuff: you'll also need to talk about feelings that may be difficult to articulate. And, you need to learn to listen as well, because communication is a two-way street. Acknowledge each other's feelings and know what is going on with your partner. Honest communication leads to trust, and without trust, you have little foundation to build upon. You must learn to compromise and resolve the inevitable conflicts that you will face. Respect and expect that you will face differences of opinion, and that it's important to respect each other's feelings.

Finally, get married for love, and do not run away from the many aspects of intimacy. Lust alone does not make for a solid relationship. Live up to your vows, and truly love each other.

*Your Voice Will Help Achieve True Equality*
In Canada before 1969, homosexual activity was considered a criminal offence. Some forty years later, same-sex marriage has become a legal reality throughout Canada (and in a few American states too). Nonetheless, many of those whom I interviewed incurred psychological damage during the intervening years, as they waited for a time when their wishes for legal status could be realized.

If you are thinking about getting married, there is little need to justify your decision. People around you can see your love, and as with the heterosexual majority, many people assume the end point of a successful courtship is marriage. It reminds me of the title of Dr Kathleen Lahey's first book: *Are We 'Persons' Yet?*.

In Canada, we finally are, as many of the battles have already been won. That does not mean everything has been accomplished, however, as there is a difference between what can be accomplished through legislation and the attitude changes needed to end prejudice and discrimination. *Your* voice will help ensure that the evolution of equality, liberty, and justice for all continues.

I hope we all get to hear you.

# How to Archive Our History

Jane Van Ingen

We all have stories to tell.

Marge McDonald was born in the Appalachian town of Nelsonville, Ohio, and moved to Syracuse, New York, in the 1950s. She wrote about her life as a lesbian and collected lesbiana. In 1986, the Lesbian Herstory Archives received a phone call and learned that Marge had recently passed away and had bequeathed her collection to the Archives. There was only one small problem. Her family became angry when they discovered that she was a lesbian, and they wanted to destroy her collection. However, the Archives found someone who got the collection to New York City. Today, the Archives are located in a brownstone in Brooklyn, and Marge's memorabilia can be found on the second floor. Visitors can see photos of Marge and her friends, look at books that Marge read and found valuable, and read her personal journals.

Be like Marge. Start a collection. Save your books, magazines, letters, emails, blogs, birthday cards, academic papers, and unpublished and/or published fiction, non-fiction, poetry, and prose. Digital photos are great, but be sure to keep printed photos of your family, friends, and lovers. Hold on to papers from conferences and organizations you may be affiliated with. Better yet, make a CD or video about your life and the issues that are important to you. Maybe you ran or currently run an organization—be it radical or mainstream. Save minutes, leaflets, bylaws, newspaper and magazine articles, brochures, flyers, correspondence, and photos. The Lesbian Herstory Archives, where I am a coordinator, has Archives of the Archives files dating back to its beginnings in 1974.

If you save newspapers or newspaper articles, be aware that piles of newspapers are a fire hazard, and newsprint becomes yellowed and deteriorates. It's far better to cut out articles you want and make photocopies of them, or print them off the Internet if the article is available online.

Store your books, papers, and keepsakes in a clean, cool, dry, dark place, as dampness, heat, and overexposure to dust and sun makes paper and electronic recordings decay. Unfold all papers so they lie flat—creases tear easily as paper ages. Remove metal staples (they rust), use plastic paper clips whenever possible, and do not use tape. The adhesive on most clear and masking tapes is acidic and damaging to paper (it's a good idea to remove tape from your documents before it is too late).

Along those lines, don't keep photographs in "stickum" photo albums because the adhesive is also acidic and will ruin your photos over time. Instead, purchase acid-free folders and sheet protectors. On the back of your photos, in soft #1 pencil, note the date of the photo and other details, including the names of the people in them. Do not use pen (the ink will seep through eventually) or labels (the glue on labels will also damage photos). Because pencil doesn't always write well on Kodak paper, you can place those photos in a sheet protector, place a label on each sheet, and describe the photo on the label.

Want to make your documents more accessible to friends and family, future generations, even … an archive? Include a timeline of the major events in your life in either written or recorded form. Be as chatty or brief as you like, then organize the collection using your outline. Identify the people whose letters appear in your collection, making clear who wrote what, and arrange the letters in order by date and/or correspondent. For a heightened level of detail, add a description of your relationship to them and other information about them. Arrange other writings, keepsakes, and clippings similarly.

Label aforementioned items with names, dates, and locations, and include information explaining how it all relates to your life. File in acid-free folders with clear headings, i.e., "Minutes from Meetings, Bears 'R' Us" or "Photos, Barbara and Kay, 1980s." And remember, things that seem obvious to you and your circle aren't—and won't be—apparent to outsiders.

Maintaining and preserving a collection can become repetitive, but don't get overwhelmed. Break the collection down to manageable portions, and devote a certain block of time—depending on how busy your schedule is—to this project. Don't chastise yourself if you get distracted and start looking at your files and photos—it happens to the best of us. Take a break and come back to it feeling refreshed.

Decide for yourself what constitutes historical importance. At the Archives, we have a special collection for Mabel Hampton, a domestic worker, entertainer, and participant in the Harlem Renaissance, which reflects her life with her partner for over forty years, Lillian Foster, her love of opera, her friendship with the Archives co-founders, and her spirituality. When she was in her eighties, she became an activist and an archivist on behalf of both gay people and African-Americans. In the early days of the Archives, she brought lesbians of all backgrounds together who loved to hear her stories. When Mabel was once asked when she came out of the closet, she replied that she was never in it! During her last days in 1989, she kept a rosary, a small pink teddy bear, and a Lesbian Herstory Archives pin by her bedside.

Maybe you have a collection of signed Judy Garland photos. Well, that's relevant, too. You would preserve those the same way you would a personal collection. Pop culture, entertainment, and sports memorabilia tell people what was important to a community at a certain time period. If there's a story behind those Judy Garland photos—maybe you got to meet her, even—then hold on to and protect whatever documentation you might have from that fabulous day.

Definitely save any matchbooks from LGBT bars or clubs, especially those that no longer exist. Joan Nestle, Archives co-founder, wrote about the bathroom line at The Sea Colony, a working-class lesbian bar in Greenwich Village in the 1950s, in her book *A Restricted Country:* "Because we were labeled deviants, our bathroom habits had to be watched ... Only one woman at a time was allowed into the toilet because we could not be trusted ... Every time I took the fistful of toilet paper, I swore eventual liberation. It would be, however, liberation with a memory." At the Archives, we have a pair of boots worn by a lesbian who marched in the NYC Dyke March, which takes place every year the day before Pride. The boots are black with red shoelaces and the American flag painted on front.

Understandably, writers, photographers, and artists don't want their work to get lost. But what about the rest of the queer community? Some volunteers at the Archives were a part of the second-wave feminism of the 1970s, ACT UP in the 1980s, and/or Lesbian Avengers in the 1990s; others are still activists. Some are librarians, fundraisers, and social workers; others are retired or on disability. But we all understand the importance of telling and preserving our stories, and that's enough.

# How to Write and Live to Tell about It

Victor J. Banis

You know who you are. Gay men, yes, but that is not what defines you for me. You are the seekers of knowledge. You email me regularly, you come up to me at workshops and book signings, sometimes you corner me at cocktail parties—always with some variation on the same unanswerable question. It is not how to live as a gay man that you want from me, which seems to me the essential question, but rather, how to write?

Of course, there are many who say the question of how to write can be answered. Browse in any bookstore. You will find entire shelves of books filled with writing advice. If you read my *Spine Intact, Some Creases*, you will discover several chapters on the subject. There are countless blogs, newsletters, workshops, seminars, and writing classes in almost any city, and plenty of them on the Internet. In theory, any one of those has the potential to turn you into a real author.

If only it were so simple. My advice in *Spine Intact, Some Creases* concludes with these remarks: "Having nattered on at such length about writing I must now say plainly what I have tried more subtly to suggest a number of times: there are no rules. There is no map. These are only signposts pointing toward a road that may not exist, leading to a land you can never reach. Have a good trip."

Does that mean the art of writing is something you can never learn? In Buddhism, for instance, it is said that you cannot learn enlightenment, it comes to you. However, you can prepare yourself for it, with study and meditation. This is true as well of learning to write. There is something to be said for hard work, for discipline, for devoting yourself to mastering the craft, the technique of writing, as in any art form. Picasso was once asked how it was that he was successful when so many other abstract artists were not.

"It's simple," he replied. "I learned to draw first."

So, yes, of course, you want to learn to draw first, you want to master the basics; grammar and spelling, of course, and plot skeleton. The first two you can get from the classic text *The Elements of Style*, the third from almost any writing class or book. And you want to work at these until they have become automatic, until you no longer have to think about them at all. It is at this point that you can practice the art of getting yourself out of the way. This is the key to enlightenment, and it is the key to the art of writing.

But this is true of life as well, isn't it? You study, you pray, you sometimes stumble, all in the interest of learning how best to live life, until hopefully you have reached a point where you no longer have to consciously think about how best to conduct yourself, in situations gay or straight. One could perhaps point you to a book or a class that would tell you how to live your life as a gay man, but, really, this would be no substitute for living it.

The art of writing is almost surely something you can never master—any more than you can ever master the art of living. Your writing is a reflection of your life. Probably the reverse is true as well. But you can prepare yourself for it, as with enlightenment. The more you learn about life, and living it, the more you will know about writing, and vice versa.

So, here are a couple of how-to's, signposts that may help you to become a better writer—and to live your life better in the process.

This first one gets left out of the writing books and the workshops too often, and that's unfortunate, really, because it just might be the most important one of all: *Have fun.*

If you're going to make it just a job, you might as well be selling shoes at Macy's. Writing is a magic carpet. Most people get one life to live, and few of them do anything more than scratch the surface of it. The writer, on the other hand, can live a score of lives, a hundred, a thousand. You can be, in your physical world, four feet tall and as ugly as a troll—but as a writer you can be Brad Pitt. The lonely housewife can be Mata Hari. You can be anyone or anything you can imagine: a courtesan, a pirate, a space traveler.

And if you're not living those lives while you are writing about them, you're not doing it right. Don't just write about a cowboy galloping across the prairie. Get on a horse and ride! And have some fun while you're at it.

But, I would say the same about being gay. Gay is hard. You catch a lot of crap. Even in these advanced times, you will almost certainly suffer discrimination; you will live with taunts, mockery, and the threat of violence. These things will not change greatly in what's left of my lifetime, or yours. Hate and ignorance are, if not eternal, surely long-lived.

But there is one thing that has been true for a long, long time, maybe since the beginning: Gays have fun. More fun than straights. It is something about our nature, that tendency to laugh at it all, to make a party out of even the most miserable of circumstances. I'm willing to bet that all the way back in the days of the cave dwellers, one of the boys was leading the others in a conga line around the campfire—and guess who he was.

So, if you asked me how to be a successful gay person, my first piece of advice would be the same as my writing advice: Have fun.

The second bit of advice I want to offer is something that gets mentioned a lot, so often that it is nearly a cliché, but it is important enough to warrant saying again: *Always give it your best shot.*

It doesn't matter if you're writing a story for an online zine that pays nothing or something for your church bulletin or a bedtime story for your children—and not just for the obvious reason, because you never know who is going to read this somewhere down the line. You want to do your best, though, for a far more fundamental reason, and this is where it mirrors life exactly: because there is no real satisfaction in doing anything half-assed.

Here is a philosophy that you can apply to your writing, and if you give it some thought, you will find that it applies just as well to your everyday life, and probably more fully to the homosexual life than to others.

When you are writing, you are out there on the stage alone. You are performing for the gods. Sing for them. Dance and leap and click your castanets. If they try to close the curtains on you, yank them open and twirl your baton out to the footlights. If they throw tomatoes, grab a couple of them and juggle them while you tap dance. If they bring out the shepherd's crook and drag you off stage, go singing "Swanee" and blowing kisses.

But, you're always alone on stage, aren't you? The big moment is always the solo. Every gay man learns that in time. Generally, a little sooner than your average straight, and a little more definitively. It's the other side of the "hard knocks" coin.

All you can do, the wisest thing you can do, is give it your best. No one, not even your maker, can ask more of you—and you should never ask less of yourself.

That's how to write. You can try it at the next party, too. Just watch out for the shepherd's crook.

# How to Survive Gay Celebrity: A Pocket Guide

Paul Bellini

*Fame: An Introduction*
So you want to be famous?

Are you certain?

Ah, how we envy celebrities. The syllogism seems to be, *Celebrities are fabulous; I am fabulous; ergo, I am a celebrity.* And when you're fabulous, the world is your oyster, even if you don't like oysters.

But let's step back and look at this objectively. Celebrities may get the best seats in restaurants, but late-night talk show hosts also publicly humiliate them. They get arrested just like anyone else, and then vilified like no one else. Is there really anything to envy? Truly, what could be more endless than fifteen minutes of fame?

As gay men, we know all too well how taxing it is to be popular. The constant burden of having to be "on" all the time. The discomfort of knowing that people are talking about you behind your back. The fact that you can't gain five pounds without precipitating a tidal wave of controversy. Celebrity is a heavy burden indeed, and even more so when you are a *gay* celebrity.

Oh, I wouldn't wish it on anyone, friends. And yet, every day, somewhere on earth, there is a young gay man with stars in his eyes. If he could only be in the same league as Judy or Liza or even Britney. Yes, and look how they turned out.

It's a double-edged sword, dear reader. Fame can also expose one's most deeply private and intimate secrets. Got a small dick? Very likely a regrettable Polaroid will surface on the Internet. Do you make meowing sounds when you're getting plowed? Once you're famous, it will be exhaustively detailed in all the tabs. This is the price you pay for renouncing anonymity. Can any mere human endure the scrutiny? No! That's why those who are famous are actually famous, because they can put up with the shit that the rest of us foist on them.

And still, many of you are not dissuaded. You are so into your own fabulousness that you can't see the hideous forest for the gorgeous trees. You insist on pursuing your God-given right to have your ass kissed for no other reason than your mug is on the cover of some magazine. Fine, so be it. The least I can do is share the wisdom gleaned from first-hand observations of others much more renowned than myself. Learn the lessons well, because once the genie is out of the bottle …

*How to Achieve Fame*

The first thing you must do is actually become famous. There are five ladders most gay men can climb in order to achieve this lofty ambition:

1. *Become a tireless self-promoter.* It doesn't matter if you are a stand-up comedian, a singer, a TV star, a radio personality, a politician, a drag queen, a drag queen running for office, a columnist for a local gay rag, a cooking show host, or just really fat and rich, celebrity requires the building and feeding of one's own myth. Unfortunately, every gay man can see right through this charade. Think you're special? Think again, bitch.

But what are you supposed to do? Hire a publicist? If you don't blow your own horn, ain't nobody gonna blow it for you, right? So you run around postering your neighborhood and circulating headshots and appearing for free on any stage or screen that will have you. You're a one-man parade! It's what you have to do. Worry about over-exposure later. The problem is, your efforts to promote yourself will ultimately backfire, for if your true talents are ever actually acknowledged warmly by the critics, everyone will still think the review was bought and paid for. It's a small community, dear.

And it's a lonely path, for the only person who can ever truly love a self-promoter is oneself.

2. *Achieve notoriety.* Kill or steal or fuck something or someone in a big splashy public way. If there's a trial, even better. Ride that notoriety up and down the courthouse steps. It helps if you're really sexy. Then everyone can have prison fantasies about you.

3. *Have greatness thrust upon you.* Sounds easy, but there are really only two ways this can happen: cure AIDS, or sue a homophobic right-wing pig and screw him in court. Odds are better in the second instance. Note that this is different from achieving notoriety, because you will be perceived as a hero. If this should ever happen to you, don your Grand Marshal hat and hop in the back of that convertible, baby.

4. *Do drag, pose nude, or transition.* The only true stars in any gay community are: a) local drag queens; b) hot guys who pose shirtless for ads; c) trannies, whose combination of brave struggle and fierce style automatically pushes them to the top of the class. The beauty of these three usually successful options is that they are visual and sexual, and therefore do not require brains or talent.

5. *Start a MySpace or Facebook page* and solicit thousands of others to be your "friends." This is the most pathetic option, but it seems to be working for a lot of young people these days. Call it virtual fame. Unfortunately, this type of fame only lasts about fifteen *seconds.*

Regardless, bear in mind that few of these options will make you rich. In fact, not even being a TV star will make you rich, at least in Canada where the boss's receptionist probably makes more than the person on screen. (Receptionist is a fine choice of occupation, by the way, if only for the access to gossip.)

*Rules of Conduct for a Gay Celebrity*
Once you have achieved gay celebrity, you must step into the world

and use it, but oh, there are many horrors ahead. Here are seven simple rules you will need to follow:

1. *Don't ever pull a fit in public, or ever leave a paltry tip.* This advice is self-evident. You may want to tell that waiter or taxi driver to fuck off, but bite your tongue. These stories always circulate and, like storm systems, they pick up speed and get worse. People in the service industry often come in contact with celebrities, and their combination of resentment and jealousy can make them vicious foes. Don't ever give a bitchy waiter anything to talk about, as the odds are good that he himself is an unemployed actor. Trust me, it's better to be known as a heroin addict than to be known as a celebrity who leaves less than twenty-five percent.

2. *Know you will be misquoted.* Sometimes this gives you a convenient excuse when you actually do say something stupid and want to disown it. But more often, your attempts to articulate something personal will be mangled by a reporter, sounding like the sort of statement only a huge asshole would make. Always rise above it, as nothing is tawdrier than writing a huffy letter correcting shoddy reportage. (While we're at it, it is also pointless to defend your work against a bitchy critic. Let it go, take a deep breath, and think about something else—for example, unique ways to kill said critic.) You will soon find out that no one really cares what you have to say. It is easier to learn to live with your own myths.

3. *Courting controversy is a booby trap.* You will be misunderstood because most people have no capacity for irony. If you pose nude as a big joke, most people will just think you're a slut. If you jokingly say you're in favor of the slaughter of baby seals, some moron will invariably say they saw you with a bloody club in your hand.

Even worse is when you actually believe what you say and make a bold statement to the gay press, such as "Gay men should stop using drugs" or "Drag is offensive to women." A bold stand is always easy for detractors to mock. Pretty soon, you'll acquire a cute nickname, like Rhonda Rehab or Butch LaBitch.

4. *Your slob days are over.* You may be the hottest thing in town right now, but do you really think people won't notice that you wear the same pair of pants every day for a week? Or that jacket with the food stains on it? Or that bird's-nest hairdo? Even the homeless try harder. Sometimes, the unavoidable happens, like when a big ugly herpetic cold sore erupts on your top lip. You do not have to be famous for this to ruin your week, but a famous person with a big ugly herpetic cold sore is definitely news for a week.

5. *Expect nothing.* Don't expect to be recognized by people, and even if they do recognize you, don't expect them to acknowledge it. If someone says, "I saw your show," never ask if they liked what they saw. Just say thanks, as though watching it was a favor they did for you. In fact, anticipate resentment. When said resentment is expressed—"Hey asshole, you think you're cool because you're a star?"—rise above it, exhibiting the dignity and grace of a Grace Kelly.

6. *Avoid groupies.* Anyone who wants to fuck you because you're famous is very likely mentally ill, prone to stalking, harassment, fake pregnancy, you name it. The groupie who will not go away won't just become your possessive lover, but very likely also your manager or agent. Even on the slightest level, it is never advisable to have sexual relations with a fan. Do not even autograph someone's penis, no matter how tempting.

Let me share with you a cautionary tale that happened to a friend of mine who was, at the time this happened, a big gay star. Star (as we shall call him) was partying in a Vancouver gay bar when a tall sexy guy said he recognized him and loved his work. A compliment like this is the equivalent to panty peeler for an insecure celebrity. Fan suggested to Star that they sneak off to a bathhouse together. But once inside, Fan had sex with just about everyone else in the place except for Star. Star felt rebuffed, insulted, and humiliated. (Hours later, when Star happened to chance upon Fan, now spent and passed out naked in his room, he felt that he just couldn't leave without saying goodbye, and he did so in the form of a big liquid autograph on sleeping Fan's back.) The moral of the story is, Star learned that Fan had taken advantage of him. (Not a lesson Fan would learn until he woke up.)

7. *Your fame goes with you everywhere you go.* Deal with the fact that you are no longer anonymous and that people will never let you forget that they know who you are. Sometimes it's fawning, sometimes it's disdain. The worst is inappropriate recognition. Most men in a bathhouse will recognize you even when you're wearing a towel and wandering around in the dark, and nothing is more disconcerting than blowing some guy who starts singing the song you turned into a hit.

To continue the previous story, when Star returned to Toronto he discovered that he would require some hassle-free treatment, if you know what I mean. Well, nothing is quite so grievous as stumbling into an STI treatment facility with a nasty dose only to have the receptionist look up and loudly proclaim, "Oh, you look fatter on TV." It's a welcome sentiment, but still, is it necessary to share it with everyone else in the room? This is a solemn reminder of two things: one, that fans come from all walks of life, including loudmouth medical receptionists; and two, that a high TVQ does not exempt one from cooties.

We can conclude that it doesn't matter if you are well known or unknown, a natural talent or a natural bore, a Mensa member or a Nazi sympathizer, as long as you have a big dick. In which case you are already a star in the gay community.

So do you still want to be famous?

Don't say you haven't been warned.

# The Do's and Don'ts of Getting Married for a Green Card

Tony Correia

*Don't do it for the wrong reasons.* "The nightlife is better" is not an excuse to marry someone. Nor is, "The guys are hotter." If there's a legitimate reason to marry someone for a green card it's that you can't get refugee status. Otherwise, if you live in a developed country with some sort of democracy/capitalist mix as a political system, you're not bad off where you are.

*Do get an AIDS test.* If you are a gay man and a woman is risking jail time and a $100,000 fine so you can be gay in the USA, then you owe it to her to get an AIDS test—you're going to have to take one for Uncle Sam anyway. The only way an HIV-positive immigrant can live in the United States is if they are married to an American citizen. Believe it or not, many women don't find out their husbands are positive until the INS interview, making for an uncomfortable drive home. Gay or straight, a status-divergent couple is a red flag for any INS agent and will add another year or two to the process. That's a lot of hand wringing. Best get it done and out of the way for both your sakes. Who knows? If you found out you were positive, you might not want to live in the States anymore.

*Don't watch the movie "Green Card".* This is a really deceiving 1990 movie starring Andie MacDowell and Gérard Depardieu (back when they were still trying to convince us he was sexy). She needs a husband to keep her apartment; he needs an American wife to stay in the country. They meet, they marry, they part, and then the INS comes calling. They reunite to rehearse their story, discover they hate each other, but their mutual appreciation for Enya conquers all and they consummate the marriage ... too late. If you do watch the movie, view it as a refracted image of reality, because there's no such thing as a forgiving INS agent.

*Do yourself a favor and tell your parents.* There is no point in signing the marriage license if you're not going to tell your parents. It doesn't take much physical evidence to prove a marriage is legitimate, but the easiest way is for the parents to be in the wedding photos. One set of parents could be absent from the ceremony, but two is cause for suspicion. There are only so many excuses for a parent not being at their child's wedding; being estranged from your parents might work for one of you but not both. As with the AIDS test, get everything out in the open. The only thing worse than not telling your parents you're married is the INS calling and telling them for you.

*Don't forget to have a real wedding.* The wedding is going to be the last best time you have before you file for resident alien status. That said, don't laugh or make faces through your vows; even shotgun weddings are romantic. Invite all your friends; better yet, invite your parents (see above). Tell your friends to treat it like a real wedding; no handmade cards written in crayon. Avoid inviting exes who are still in love with either of you and who might want to use your wedding for some sort of vendetta. Send real invitations with real RSVPs. If you "elope," go somewhere romantic to do it—nothing says "marriage of convenience" like a Vegas wedding. Make sure the ring is gold, and remember—people who wear wedding bands have a tan line on that finger.

*Do get a lawyer.* Getting married for a green card without a lawyer is like buying a house without a real estate agent; you can do it, but one wrong move and you can get screwed for a lifetime. Immigration lawyers do not want to know the marriage is phony. It's good practice to keep up the act for the lawyer; the INS is going to be much worse. Do everything the lawyer tells you to do; don't question the lawyer's advice when it comes to what the INS requires of you. Give the lawyer something to work with. A lawyer is there to file forms and act as a witness; only you can convince the INS you're a straight couple.

*Don't kid yourself; you're married.* It takes two to commit perjury. If you can't live with the person you're getting married to, then it's probably not a good idea to marry him or her. Marriage is more than just knowing the color of your spouse's underwear; it's knowing what he eats for breakfast, her routine, who his friends are, and what annoys her about you. Married people share bank accounts and credit cards; they are the benefactors of life and health insurance policies; their mail goes to the same address. If you cannot trust your spouse with a credit card, then can you trust them not to sell you out to the INS? Your spouse will also annoy you like a real spouse would. However much you may pretend otherwise, you are legally bound to each other. Divorce will cross your mind several times before it's over. The words, "Nothing is worth this!" will cross your lips. Avoid movies such as *Strangers on a Train* and *The Postman Always Rings Twice.* Use common sense and ask for a prenuptial agreement; you know how this is going to end.

*Do your homework; rehearse what you're going to say.* Never stop polishing your act. From the moment you decide to get married, re-enact how you met, your first date, first kiss, and when you started living together. Stick as close to the truth as you possibly can; once you start moving into the realm of fantasy, the larger the margin of error come crunch time. Make sure there is something intimate about your story: the name of a bottle of wine; the color of the sky; a turn of phrase—something only the two of you would know. Be careful when letting friends help with the rehearsal process—everyone wants to be a director. Again, avoid letting exes participate, this will only work against you. Make sure your stories are exactly the same; if one of you strays, it's curtains.

*Don't separate.* Once you have applied for permanent residency there is no going back. Even if you divorce, you have to go through the interview process. It is important that once you are married, you and your spouse stay as joined at the hip as possible. It's not unusual for couples to be apart for the purposes of a job or school, but the INS won't see it that way. You can't blame them. If you do separate for an extended period of time, make sure there's a legitimate reason, like a family emergency.

*Do be prepared to wait.* Even if you survive the interview process there is no guaranteeing how long it will take for you to get your green card. Even before 9/11 it could take nearly two years after your interview. Since many of the 9/11 terrorists were in the country on legitimate visas, one can only imagine how much more scrutiny must go into every card. When you do get your card, prepare to be underwhelmed. You will think, "All that for this?" Then be prepared to guard it with your life.

*Don't do it.* There's only one reason to get married: Love.

# How to Bury Our Dead

## Amber Dawn

Have you ever had to attend a Catholic or Sikh or Japanese or Irish funeral and felt a little uncertain about the cultural grieving practices? We can all thank cyberspace for easy-to-find funeral etiquette. Simply visit Wikipedia before you do something tactless, like sending flowers to a Jewish funeral service.

Now try doing a search for "queer funeral etiquette" and Wikipedia will tell you that "no page with that title exists.'" Try Googling it. The closest result is a website that explains tipping etiquette for gay men vacationing in Mexico.

It only gets worse if you swap labels and mix up words. The first result on a search for "gay memorial service" brought me to an article about the cancellation of a Navy veteran's funeral because his church congregation learned that he was gay. If you search for the same article you will discover that this happened in—yes—2007.

Everyone dies; we can agree on that. And although we probably don't really like to, we can also agree that the mortality rate for queers is higher than for happily married heterosexuals. Doesn't it seem a little off that we—with our rich array of community rituals and traditions—don't have customary means to mourn? Exactly how do we bury our dead?

I am not an expert. All of my grieving I've done in rather bitter privacy. I can only share with you my stories of bereavement in hopes that they help spark conversation, and that conversation brings change. I believe this is the way we queer folks do things.

I'll start us off with what I know—my family is made up of mostly hard-working farmers, churchgoers, and strong believers in heaven.

I was seven years old when I attended my first funeral. My Great Uncle Dave lived with his wife, Dottie, on a corn and chicken farm until he died of a heart attack before fifty. My ma made a bed for me in the back seat of the Volkswagen Rabbit and drove without stopping from Fort Erie, Ontario to Auburn, New York. Her good black dress hung in the back passenger-side window, a funeral garb curtain that blocked the sun as I dozed away the five-hour drive.

When we arrived, Dave and Dottie's frame house was still as huge and white as ever. The corn still stood in dutiful rows. Willow trees sprawled across the front lawn, still waiting for grandkids and cousins to climb them. Dottie's mean-tempered geese chased me up the driveway, hissing, like they always had done.

My ma led me to the back door—because family never came through the front—and into the mudroom where Uncle Dave's flannel shirts crowded the coat tree. I watched her gulp back a grievous sob as she searched for an empty hook for my red wool poncho. Growing up with a single mom, I had seen plenty of tears. Mamma wasn't one to hide her most recent dating disaster or debt struggles. But this was different. This sounded as if something had been dislodged deep in the combines of her body. Her crying fired up loudly and continued, almost mechanically, as we were received by a half-dozen or so aunties, passed around the kitchen from one set of open arms to the next.

What I learned about funerals that day: You get to keep your (Sunday) shoes on inside the house. Cake and pie arrives in landslides. No one jabbers when the priest stays to drink with the family. Well-recited stories are told about when the departed either comically injured or humiliated themselves, or both. You cry whenever the crying comes. Maybe it's when your second cousin, Holly, hugs you so tight and uncomfortably long that you feel her faux-pearl necklace denting your forehead. Maybe it's when you're in the living room, where the open casket lay for three days, forcing yourself to look at the pale and gentle flesh of your uncle's closed eyelids. And when you cry it's uncensored. And you're not alone.

It's likely we all have a story something like this: a memory of bagpipes or a parade of black suits or kneeling so long that your feet fall asleep. I wonder if our memories could be the key to shaping queer funerals? Conquering and compiling the fine details like the unearthly quiet of a receiving room or how particularly buttery the sweets tasted. Or in my case how much the tattooist's gun burned on my back.

I mourned my first queer death in a tattoo shop. There's a scarlet-haired, rock-n-roll vixen on my back. She peeks out of my shirt collar and runs, right of my spine, down towards my hip. I clenched my fists (and my jaw and my butt cheeks) for nearly eight hours before the tattooist was finished.

She attracts a lot of attention, my tattoo. Especially from biker types who don't have any qualms about touching a perfect stranger's back. "Nice ink," they say. Some have even gone as far as sliding my tank top to the side to get a better look. So when they ask, "What made you get that?" I feel a certain vindication when I tell them, "It's a memorial tattoo for a lover. She was nineteen when she died."

The conversation usually ends there.

If I were to continue, I'd say I picked up a phone call from a friend sometime in the late fall of 1993. This friend and I hadn't spoken since high school and she didn't waste words asking how I was doing all the way out in Vancouver. Her news was swift as a kick: Val overdosed in her parent's rec room. The "immediate-family-only" service had already passed. Her obituary had already run in the Niagara local papers.

"But I didn't even know she moved home," was the only response I could come up with. It was true, it must have been at least a year since I had seen her.

"Well," my friend sighed, sounding impatient. "She came back to get clean."

I went to my old dealer's house—the one with the Confederate flag in the bay window and the stupid smoke that couldn't find its way out of the living room—and I told everyone there. Some lay unmoving on the many ragged sofas jammed into the tiny apartment and slept through the news. Some had never met Val and shrugged in careless sympathy. I stuck around for the three or four people who called Val a friend—despite the fact that the second-hand freebase coke smoke was making me ill and also making me crave coke

We told stories:

Remember how we used to cut class to swim in the gorge? Remember tobogganing on garbage-bag sleds at Sugar Bowl Park? Remember Black Label beer and our secret drinking spot near Devil's Hole: how'd we manage not to kill ourselves climbing drunk down to those caves?

After we exhausted the tales of high school, the road trip sagas began. How Val could neither read a map nor stay awake at the wheel. But she could find a radio station, even in the butt-fuck-nowhere prairies where nothing but tall grass lives. And she knew the words to every classic rock song from "Abracadabra" to "Ziggy Stardust."

From these stories I omitted the part when Val tucked my hands under her bomber jacket, held them against her bare belly until my fingers were warm in the November night. Our first kiss we had ducked between two parked cars in a bowling alley parking lot. I used to chew my lips raw daydreaming about when we'd kiss again. I noticed things about her that made me light-headed and confused, like she always wore such short skirts that if she sat on a vinyl chair she'd leave a faint sweat imprint of her thighs. I struck these tales from our impromptu memorial because Val and I were the only ones who knew. Now that she was dead, I was the only one.

The lack of "out" funerals has been going on long before I lost a loved one. In 1987, Cleve Jones and a group of San Franciscan LGBT activists began the AIDS Memorial Quilt, an enormous and ever-growing observance to the lives of people who have died of AIDS-related causes. In the late '80s, most of the people who died with AIDS, or more to the point, the gay men who died with AIDS, were denied a memorial service because funeral homes and cemeteries refused to take their remains. The Quilt was one of the only places where surviving loved ones could formally remember and grieve.

If you visit the *aidsquilt.org* website you'll notice that the Names Project Foundation has honorably chosen to use the site as an educational tool and an affirming celebration of life. Click the "make a panel" button. You can read over the encouraging guidelines to submitting to the quilt. Everything from hand-embroidery to spray paint art is welcome. The only specific requirement is the dimensions: six feet by three feet. If you didn't know the history, it might not occur to you that this is the size of a human grave, a heed to the time when we had to bury our dead in cloth coffins of our own creation.

As a kinky, genderqueer femme with a big mouth and what you could call a rather enterprising pussy, I am accustomed to having to create my own family, my home and community, and even myself. I am proud of the keen ability queer folks have to create personal, joyful somethings out of the nothings we're all-too-often offered. I don't know, however, if I can be proud that we've had to make our own coffins.

In addition to the tattoo shop, I've also grieved in gay bar bathrooms, in a New Orleans-bound van full of traveling burlesque dancers, and at a massage parlor staff room. This may sound delightfully renegade—but really, where else are we to hold a queer service? Annual memorials and days of remembrance have been an answer to this. Often housed at progressive university campuses or hosted by social justice groups, these mass memorials allow us to remember our own. Or at least they try to.

In spring 2003, I was working at a garishly decorated "rub-n-tug" next to the King George Highway. It was a bad month for business and some girls started working double shifts or hitting the stroll on Richards Street after the massage parlor closed for the night to keep from going broke. It is times like those that I was thankful to be a penniless homosexual artist who could live happily on a couple of weekly dates with regular clients.

Whenever business was slow, the staff inevitably grew louder. We perfected our booty shake to blaring loud hip hop, smoked marijuana until we broke into giggle fits, and killed hours bitching on the phone to other working girls at other massage parlors about how business was slow. So when I showed up to a dead silent workplace one day in May I knew something was wrong. I walked down the vacant hallway, past the row of empty massage studios, to the staff room where I found Summer with her head crumpled into her hands. The other girls all stared at the floor. Summer was no crybaby; she's a high school drop-out, single mom, her baby's daddy was murdered, her boyfriend was in provincial prison up North.

"Who died?" I asked, gravely.

"Shelby, fuck. You remember Shelby. Chinese. Tranny. Worked by the name of Ling. You know that older Asian girl. She was done all the way around."

*Done all the way around* was Summer's crude phrasing to note that Shelby was a post-operative transsexual. I did remember her. She worked downtown alongside the high track, big money girls. Summer said the word on Shelby was she was cut into pieces and left in a shopping cart outside a laundromat.

For the days that followed, we watched the local news and brought the papers to work. We didn't hear anything about Shelby; no obituary and no funeral—it was as if Shelby had never existed. I was left wondering how it happened. I couldn't help but think that Shelby was targeted because of gender. Gender, race, and occupation, I was certain, were the reasons for the lack of media coverage. After about a week we decided to light a candle and say a prayer in the staff room and move on.

Six months later, I was given a flyer for the Transgender Day of Remembrance. Each year there is a memorial to remember the transgender people across North America and the world who have died. Multiple cites have been observing the Transgender Day of Remembrance since 1999. Over the years it has grown from small DIY gatherings to well-publicized and attended events. I wondered if Shelby would be among those being remembered: I prayed that she would be.

I invited Summer to come with me and mourn. She eyed the memorial's flyer, with its activist jargon, and saw that it was being held at a university campus. "Not my thing," she said and handed the flyer back to me.

I went alone. As I entered the crowded campus classroom, my chest tightened. There were many familiar faces: college queers, forefathers and mothers of local trans activism; there was even a member of parliament. More people than seating space, they stood along the back wall, crouched in front of the speakers' table. Seeing them all suddenly made Shelby's death more real. Overwhelmed, I squatted on the newly carpeted floor close to the exit.

I had a short eulogy that I wanted to share. I wanted to let people know Shelby was a strong woman; that, with all respect, she was a tough-ass bitch. From what I knew of her, she never hid nor compromised who she was. It couldn't have been easy working alongside of pimps and rows of nineteen-year-old girls for hire. I also wanted to invite anyone in the room who knew Shelby to share a story or two.

I did not get an opportunity to say any of this. The memorial quickly turned into a political meeting, a soundboard for topics such as surgery funding, the recently disbanded gender clinic, and trans inclusion in the Bill of Human Rights. A short documentary about San Francisco's Day of Remembrance was screened. I remember growing anxious at about this time; I watched one of the speakers struggle with the borrowed film projector and began to wonder when we were going to read the names. When were we going to remember our dead?

I was visibly fidgeting when the list of names were finally brought out and passed around. Each person present took one name from the list. One by one the names of the deceased and circumstances of the deaths were read out loud, mostly women's names and mostly violent deaths. I heard someone say, "My name is Shelby Tom, I worked as a prostitute in Vancouver, Canada. I was forty years old when I was murdered, allegedly by a client. My body was found in a shopping cart in North Vancouver."

A loud wail escaped my lips and I buried my head into my legs to prevent more from coming out. No one else was crying out loud, so I figured the appropriate thing to do was keep my head down until I felt my jeans grow damp with tears. I was still crying when an abrupt announcement was made that time had run out, the university was closing, and we needed to leave.

Campus security ushered us out the doors. I moved along in a slow, dizzy line as people looked at me with pity. I believe a woman asked if I'd be all right. I believe she had a soft-butch haircut and a bike helmet and maybe even was someone I knew. When she hugged me I held my breath, determined not to cry all over her. I was embarrassed about my uncontainable and seemingly peerless emotion. I have not since been to a Transgender Day of Remembrance.

Make two lists. One of queers you've know who have died. Another of queer funerals you've attended. How do they compare? As you probably gathered, my first list is a whole lot longer. What I've learned about queer funerals is—they don't exist. Worst-case scenario, we are forced back into the closet at our funerals. At best, our deaths become political, platforms for public education and human rights lobbying. They become measures of the work that still needs to be done in this world. And once again, I am proud to be a part of a community that in the face of death rolls up its sleeves and says *we've got a job to do*. At the same time, at risk of sounding enfeebled, it's just not fair. How truly sad it is to not be afforded a funeral!

So I have no expert advice on "how to bury your dead" because I've never actually done it. But that doesn't mean I haven't imagined an old country farmhouse filled with queer folk who have gathered to properly grieve. Maybe you can imagine it too. Picture Mac jackets and faux-fur and good leather hung in the mudroom. You come in through the back door because family never comes through the front, and you are family. You can hold your partner's hand the whole time until your fingers grow numb if you want to. The stories shared here are uncensored, including the ones that take place in bathroom stalls or parked cars. Photos, taken at Pride Parade or Faerie Camp or the bar, make their way around the room. When you are handed the photo of yourself—you with the loved one you came to mourn—stare down at it until the colors start to blur and you find yourself whispering, "Thank you, thank you, thank you." And when you're ready, go bravely into the living room where the casket lies. Take as long as you need; this moment is yours to say goodbye. Imagine this last look. Imagine hair and hands, eyelashes and lower lip, and all the memories that a body holds.

Our lives are worth the fruit baskets and raisin cakes. We are worth calla lilies and pink roses. We're worth stone or scattering ashes. Hymn and song. Wine and ritual. Surely we've all earned hours of storytelling. And most certainly our lives are worth the tears.

# How to Throw a Women's Playparty

## Elaine Miller

So you want to throw a sex or dungeon party. Whether you live in a small town or a bustling queer metropolis, a lot of the things that can go wrong and should go right about a party are the same. I'm speaking here of throwing a big party for a lot of women in a public venue, because that's what I've been doing for the last decade. But you can easily scale the operation down to fit into your living room, or a big tent in the desert, or your grandmother's house while she's on that Mediterranean cruise.

Um. Forget I said that last part.

*The Two "Who's"*

As with any party, the people involved are the most important (and delightful) ingredient. There are two "who's" to consider: who's helping and who's invited.

If you're throwing a small- to medium-sized party, or if you have nothing else to do but organize events, then one person, with volunteer help, can set up a splashy good time. But if you're doing something really big, you'll need more dedicated help. And since this is a women's event, you're looking at forming a committee.

Choose your co-organizers carefully. A wide range of skills is best: Someone handy with tools, someone handy with the Internet, someone handy with people, and so on. Everyone should agree to see the event through to the end, in a professional manner, and without drama. Everyone should know what they are capable of committing in terms of time and energy, and what part of the event they are ultimately responsible for. It's good to have an agreement that a committee member who is falling behind will ask for help. Finding out the day before the party that the promotional materials did not make it out to the streets creates a certain pain—and it's not the delightful pain of a riding crop. All financial issues should be discussed before you make your pact. Who fronts the money for expenses? When do they get paid back? What happens to the income from the party itself? Who is responsible if the party fails to make costs back? How are records kept?

Okay. Your fellow organizers (not too many of them, now!) are committed. They're skilled. They're realistic. They've been briefed on what to expect. And they can get along. Since I've already decided for you that the type of event you're putting on is a kinky sex party for women, you move on to the next step, the volunteers.

Most parties allow volunteers to enter the event for free, in return for a certain number of hours of volunteer labor. How much labor depends on what type of event. For a single night's party, more than an hour and less than two often works out fine.

Choosing volunteers first from among your closest community is a reasonable thing to do, as you'll need to count on them to be true to their word about showing up and performing the duties you've assigned. A sprinkling of friendly strangers leavens the mix, so be prepared to publicize a call for volunteers. You meet some wonderful people that way. An organizer should be responsible for scheduling volunteer shifts and for making sure she has contact info for every volunteer.

Who to invite to a queer women's playparty? Women, of course! You should find plenty of women in the local dyke community, but don't forget our bisexual queer sisters. Remember, outreach is rewarding in so many ways. The definition of "woman" is left as an exercise for you. Think carefully, grasshopper, and be prepared to publicly explain your choice of definitions.

*Make a Date*
Choose a date that works for you. Do some research to avoid, if you can, major religious holidays, days when similar events are being held in your city, and days when no one will come to a party.

*Location and Venue*
A single organizer should be chosen to deal with the venue managers, and all venue-related communications before, during, and after the party should flow through them. Be honest and upfront with venue providers about what sort of event you're holding. Not the nitty-gritty "I'm planning on beating last season's record of thirty orgasms in a row!" but a more businesslike "We are a professional organization that holds events of a sex-positive nature for women. Everything we do is legal, safe, and clean." If you live in the Bible belt, however, you might need to lie, cheat, and obfuscate to get your venue, which is outside the scope of this essay.

Pick a venue that's easy and inexpensive to get to, or one that's in an area that people are already used to visiting, such as downtown or the center of your city's queer community. If you have to include a map to the area as well as to the exact street, you'll lose eighty percent of your partygoers to armchair inertia ("I wanted to go, but it seemed like so much work"). And while we're talking about making it accessible to partygoers, make it Accessible, too. Sexy, kinky women with disabilities are a real and vibrant part of our community. Don't forget that some spaces that say they're accessible are only marginally so, especially with regard to the bathrooms. If you're not familiar with the needs of folks with disabilities, ask for advice.

If you're lucky enough to have the riches of *several* possible accessible venues, by all means consider the ambiance of each space before you make your decision. Imagine the space filled with groups of women in leather and costumes, sexy dresses, and smart suits.

Imagine where women will walk, sit, converse, flirt, cruise, play, and fuck. Pick the one that feels right to you.

*Pre-party Planning*

Once you have picked a venue, pay a preliminary planning visit. Think about how human traffic will flow, and roughly imagine how furniture, supply stations, social areas, and concessions will fit into the space. Draw a map or take pictures, sketch reminders to yourself, or, heck, just walk through looking at everything—*if* you have perfect recall and the ability to describe, six weeks later, how well a medical table might fit in that corner. Make a note of the lighting and sound system, the heat and cooling, where the electrical outlets are, the fire extinguishers, and the various exits. How will the venue look when you arrive to set up for the party, and how do they expect it to look when you leave? What is the maximum capacity? What time can you enter the space to set up on the day? Are there things that will need to be moved out before you can bring in dungeon furniture? Where is the ladder kept? The garbage cans? Is there a sink or drain near where you'll put the concession? Will you need to bring in tables for the door people? What about coat check? Are you allowed to sink great big eyebolts into the ceiling?

*Tickets and Prices*

How much will you charge for the event? If it's too expensive, many women won't be able to afford it, and you'll attract criticism for being a heartless capitalist. Too cheap, and you'll go broke on expenses. Will you have a sliding scale? Make an estimate of your costs, decide how many women will be able to pay to come, and you'll have an idea of the minimum you'll need to charge. Try to find out what other similar events are charging.

If you're selling advance tickets, you'll need to print numbered ones. Make sure it's hard to make illicit copies. You'll need to convince a few stores to carry tickets for you. In the case of online sales, you'll need to have an up-to-date will-call list at the door and be able to shut off sales once you print your final list of names. With all advance sales, your door person will need to know how many tickets were sold so you know how many unticketed women you can let in before—oh, magic words—you are sold out.

*Get the Word Out*

If you're having a private, invitation-only party, do invite people individually, with a personal message, rather than in one mass email. You might consider allowing those well known to you the privilege of inviting others, and restrict acquaintances to bringing a single date and not a posse. A strict RSVP will be necessary for your entry list.

If you're having a public party, your city and your political climate will inform your decisions about where and how to publicize. As a rule, though, your local queer newspaper is good, and your local right-wing Christian newspaper is bad. Local fetish stores, queer bars, the coffee shop where every dyke goes, and the queer bookstore are all good places to poster. Small handbills may be handed out at similar events or conferences in the time preceding the party. Paid print ads might be necessary.

Your event should have its own informative web page, and all materials can refer to that for further details. The various social networking websites can prove useful in disseminating information, as can on-topic local mailing lists. If you spam, however, you will earn yourself some very bad press. Publicize wisely.

If you're planning more than a single party, encourage party guests to give you their email address (keep a clipboard at the door that guests can sign).

## Setting up on Party Day

The party setup takes the most effort—and uses a lot of volunteers. Provide bottled water, perhaps a big jug of coffee, and don't break out the doughnuts until you've all got a considerable amount of work done. Don't forget a full tool kit, a flashlight, and supplies like staples, tape, and twine. A bunch of extension cords and multi-plug power bars will make your life easier.

Assign each organizer an area of responsibility, have a rough action plan, and then assign each volunteer to a specific area to set up. Time is of the essence, because everyone wants a chance to get all polished up before the party starts.

## BDSM Equipment

One of the most labor-intensive parts of throwing a dungeon party is the transportation and setup of furniture and equipment. Unless you have a dedicated venue with existing furniture, you'll need to rent a truck to pick up equipment, and, at the end of the party, return it all.

The amount and type of dungeon furniture you'll need depends on the exact type of party you're pitching, what's available in your city, and what will fit in your venue. Here's a list of ideas: a sling, a St. Andrew's cross, a sturdy padded platform, a spanking bench, a suspension frame, a cage, a sensory deprivation location, places for fucking (mattresses, pillows), spots for aftercare and cuddling, a medical/mess play area (bright lighting and plastic drop cloth), and whatever theme areas suit your party. Wrestling? Body painting? Lingerie?

If you're insane (in the good way, of course) and have a bit of time and some cash, you can build some sex/BDSM furniture. Plans are readily available on the Internet. Storing the furniture afterward should be easy—anyone would be delighted to have a bondage cross in her living room.

*Safer Sex and Cleaning*
A good host always offers condoms, gloves, and lube, as well as appropriate cleaning supplies: disinfectant in spray bottles for furniture; rubbing alcohol for people; and paper towels. I would add plastic drop cloths, clean sheets, clean towels, a basket for dirty laundry, and one garbage can per safer sex station. A folding TV table makes a great supplies station. You'll need a few stations for a large party—someone who's beginning a scene should be able to see one when she looks around.

*The Concession Stand*
All playparties need water and snacks. You may decide to hand these out free of charge or sell them. If you're selling, don't forget a float and a cashbox. You may go all fancy and cater trays of veggies or simply sell potato chips and doughnuts. You may offer pop and juice. Keep cold things cold, even if you're simply using a bin with ice. And don't forget to have a variety of snacks, so a diabetic woman with wheat allergies can play hard and then get her blood sugar back up, and so a vegan isn't stuck with pork rinds or nothing.

Decide whether you'll offer alcohol at your playparty, based on your own best opinions, the common etiquette of your crowd, and the municipal regulations in your city. If you do, you'll need to arrange for a license or allow the venue to sell, which may affect your rental fees. Be aware of the many extra problems brought on by tipsy players, and that a liquor license often markedly restricts what you can legally do ... such as be naked and touching others. Which, after all, is what your party is about.

*Atmosphere*
Decor makes a difference. You get to decide what your party looks like, but it should look like something not strictly ordinary. Acquire whatever you need for decorating well ahead of time. Do you want

conversation areas separate from play areas, or all mixed in? Do you want clear sight lines, or will a woman have to move to a different area if she wants to cruise that cute dyke with the crewcut? Give some thought to the magical, sexy, permissive space you're creating—people will always notice the effort you put in.

## Lighting

You have to pay damn close attention to lighting when you're creating a mood, and if it's wrong, folks will be much less likely to feel sexy. You'll need some bright spots for medical, piercing, or cutting scenes. You'll need some dimly lit spots for cuddling and fucking, except for the exhibitionists, who will want spotlights. Overhead fluorescent lighting should be strictly avoided. But you knew that.

## Tunes

Anything you pick for music will immediately be vetoed by a vociferous bunch of opinionated women, and just as vigorously defended by another bunch. Don't sweat it, as you really can't please everyone. Unless you have a live DJ who knows her sex-party stuff, just make the soundtrack as close to hands-off and error-free as you can, and don't let an overemphatic dance beat cause impromptu synchronized flogging shows.

## Welcoming Your Guests

Your door volunteer, picked for having the friendliest smile and most flirtatious manner, will need a cash float, a way to count heads, the comp list, the will-call list, and if she's got a copy of the oft-consulted volunteer schedule, you'll always know where one is, won't you? If you are asking people to sign a document that says they're adult women who are going to see consensual sex and SM, and they're not going to sue you if they get a sliver from the spanking bench, then you'll need a pile of waivers, and somewhere to stash the signed ones. A few printed sets of party rules should be available, too, and new arrivals can be invited to peruse them.

### Being the Host

As the party host, it's your job to make people welcome. Smile. Mingle. Be enthusiastic about meeting new people, and feel free to introduce people to each other. If you spot someone off by herself looking unhappy, consider approaching her and doing a friendly check-in. The host of a party does a lot to set the tone, so do it consciously. Sometimes that also means being the first to strip your clothes off, or the first to start a scene in the middle of the room.

### Playfulness Rules

Adjust the rules to the needs of the venue and the legalities of your area, but try to keep the main rules few and clear, and concentrate on helping everyone have fun within those simple guidelines. "Please do" keeps the party going, while "You can't do that" kills the sexy. Dungeon monitors should be experienced, sensible, and of a helpful rather than dictatorial nature. I can't stress that enough.

### Thank You

When your afterglow (and exhaustion) have faded, make sure you thank the people at the venue, the volunteers, the ticket vendors, and the people who donated furniture and time and trucks and bondage gear and Pride flags. Keep the goodwill flowing; you'll need it, because it's already time to start planning the next event. Ready? Set! Go!

# Ten Principles for the Good Gay Man

## Jay Starre

1. *Out Not Others*

You are gay.

This is a part of you, but does not define you, not entirely. The same can be said of others. Let them choose for themselves how they wish to see who they are. Every person is unique in how they express their sexuality. Express your sexuality as freely as possible, while allowing others the benefit of their own private or public expression.

Allow them to choose their own manner and timing of speaking out about their sexuality.

2. *Put Promiscuity in Perspective*

The word sounds archaic and judgmental. And so are some of our attitudes as individuals and as a society.

You need to put it in perspective. Sex is an intimate act and fraught with emotion, even if you don't often pay attention to your feelings or those of others.

The physical risks of sex with a parade of strangers are obvious, but the emotional risks are not so apparent. You will do yourself or others no favor by ignoring them.

Moderation is not a bad thing, and quality over quantity is something to consider. The astronomical number of your conquests does not say anything about your attractiveness or quality as a person. Ugly trolls and assholes often get a lot of sex, even if it's just with other ugly trolls and assholes.

3. *Know the Truth about Barebacking*

There is nothing wrong with barebacking; it is not a sin.

But it is risky. It can lead to STDs. It can mean you have to live with HIV the rest of your life. Make your choices with consideration for the future. Get tested. Be honest. Condoms may be a little trouble, but don't make the decision not to use them just because you feel like being lazy.

### 4. Let Go of Judgments

He's too fat, he's too much of a bear, he's kinky, a slut, a tranny, straight, HIV positive. Do you say these things to yourself? Do others offer these judgments to you or about you or about others?

True character, true friendship, and true love regularly obliterate those self-imposed walls of judgmental discrimination. Look beyond the surface and you may find something much more meaningful. You may find a real person, unlabeled and worth knowing.

### 5. Support a Gay Agenda

Gay businesses, gay politics, gay charities, gay arts, gay friends. Do your share in helping create a culture of pride and support. You probably won't win a toaster for coming out, but you'll enjoy a sense of solidarity while having some fun along the way. Be a friend to gays and gay culture.

### 6. Be Proud

Being gay is a wonderful, exciting, adventurous journey, but it neither makes you better nor worse than anyone else.

You should not be apologizing for who you are, unless you really don't like yourself. And if you don't like yourself, give change a try. If others don't like you, try to understand why, and then deal with it.

Give yourself a break. Give yourself credit for your accomplishments or your acts of kindness.

Be proud of your soul and your heart, which are yours alone and no one else's.

## 7. *Deal with Substance Abuse and Addictions*

If you need a drink or a toke or some crystal to enjoy yourself or get off, or you can't have good sex without getting high first, you are addicted and need help. Life is pretty damn fine even without drugs, and there are plenty of ways to enjoy the day without getting high. Drugs are easy to take, easier than working for that pleasure you want. Drugs are hard to shake. Asking for help is scary, and failure in beating addiction is common, but you can't get anywhere if you don't try.

Smoking cigarettes, drinking too much alcohol, eating more than you really want or need—there are all kinds of addictive behaviors that intrude on a creative, happy life. Look to your behaviors and deal with them.

Remember that you are not a scumbag for being addicted. To err is to be human. To strive to improve yourself is a daily task. Freeing yourself from addiction in some form is just part of the common human path.

## 8. *Explore Love, Relationships, and Marriage*

You are gay, for God's sake, and don't need to fit your love life into some pre-conceived cultural idea of what is right and what is wrong. Please yourself, and if a relationship is what you want and need, go for it.

If you want a relationship that is monogamous, or crave that one special guy to love and cherish above all others, or simply want to love someone and be loved yourself, don't think it's impossible. It could be difficult, a lot of work, even traumatic and disappointing. But a life without love is pretty empty, even if in the end you only learn to love yourself. Love is not a nasty word.

Love is an entirely natural emotion common to all humans, gay or straight, male or female. Love is not for the faint-hearted or reserved, nor is it only for the wimpy or sentimental. In fact, raunchy sex can be incredibly hot with someone you love, the love element raising the bar beyond what most illegal substances claim to deliver. Love is truly an aphrodisiac.

Relationships are undeniably complicated, but without question rewarding. Relationships come in many flavors, and marriage is one of those delicious options. If you want to get married to another man, do it. It may not be legal in your state or country, but it is legal somewhere, and if you want it bad enough, go there and get married.

As far as love and relationships go, don't be afraid to declare and live your beliefs. They're yours.

### 9. Respect Yourself

This is the key to all choices in life. You won't end up doing things you shouldn't have, or you wish you hadn't done, if you simply think too highly of yourself to allow them to happen. You would never beat a child, or steal from your mother, or cheat a friend if you learn to respect yourself. Once you've learned that, it is easier to take the next step, which is learning to respect others.

### 10. Be Not Afraid

There will always be someone who spits out the word "faggot." They may shout it at you, or at someone you know, or even at a stranger on the street in your presence. Shit happens.

Don't be afraid of that cruelty. Understand it. Face it. Stand up to it. Let it pass you by like the empty whisper of ancient prejudices. It is nothing.

Don't let fear of that condemnation or physical threat turn you aside from being who you are.

Embrace yourself. Be not afraid.

# Fifty Suggestions for the Aftermath

## Achy Obejas

1. Let her go. Don't be selfish. You've done enough harm already.
2. Let her say whatever she needs to say, and just agree. Consider it a gesture on your part.
3. Don't let her have the last word.
4. Don't be dramatic—just walk away. You're not injured royalty; you can't order armies to act in revenge.
5. Don't ignore the evidence, the reasons this had to happen: You lied. You proved yourself untrustworthy. Don't even attempt to explain why you were still planning a future only four months ago. Don't say you were trying.
6. Don't ignore the evidence: You have a history, a pattern. Every beginning overlaps an ending.
7. Don't ignore the evidence: You love a good pain-and-pleasure cocktail.
8. Admit you were bored. The last time she tried to tell you about her hopes and dreams, your mind kept wandering back to *To Have and Have Not*, the movie in which Bogart meets Bacall, and Bacall says, "You remember how to whistle, don't you?" and you were thinking it felt a bit like *Casablanca*, and also that Martinique seemed very clean, very tidy on the screen.
9. It's okay to say you couldn't keep up. You tried at first— secretly downloading songs she and her friends sang that you'd never heard, learning the words when she wasn't around, rehearsing recipes while she was at work that you could act blasé about later, upping your routine to three reps

and twice the weight. But your knees hurt every time you went running together, and it got so you couldn't hide the pain though you were going through Percocets like M&Ms, and you don't like Vietnamese cuisine (the fish sauce will always make you think of your uncle's war stories, the way he waddles because of the metal in his ankle), and the truth is you don't have the context for the songs.

10. Recognize that you fought constantly. Everything was about tone. The last time you said, "Hey ..." while sleepily reaching for her under the sheets, she came back at you hard: "What does that mean?" You jerked. "What? What?" she demanded. And you imagined tree snails shriveled by a deluge of salt.

11. Consider that you never *really* fought. Ever. Whenever you tried to provoke a fight, she'd "understand." She even understood when you grabbed her, lifted her wholly, and threw her against the wall. She was shaken, certainly, but she reached out and engulfed you, stroked your hair and the place where your neck and shoulders meet, a mess of kisses.

12. Make her talk to you.

13. Kiss her, but not on the lips.

14. Shut up. You'll only make it worse. What good will it do to tell her about the night with the soldier in Munich? It was only one night. And you never kissed him. Although for years you carried that image of him leaning over you, aroused, his belly softer than you'd suspected, arms trembling with effort ... and you evoked it whenever you needed a little nudge, a little push.

15. Stop saying, "I love you" at the end of your phone calls; drop the word "love" when you sign off on your emails to her.

16. Give her some space. You don't get to make it okay by trying to apologize, by forcing the apology. You don't even mean it.

17. Maneuver a meeting.
18. Pretend you're fine.
19. Pretend you don't care.
20. Pretend that it hurt and you miss her and question that decision every minute of every day.
21. Confess.
22. Make her confess.
23. Send her a gift, something small and sweet: an orange cupcake, maybe a ceramic dolphin.
24. Call her.
25. Delete her number from your phone. It's best that way, and you know it.
26. Stop looking at her web page.
27. The next time you pray, be as specific as you can be about what you want and need.
28. The next time you pray, wish her well.
29. Wish that she gets exactly what she deserves.
30. Reconsider everything.
31. Cry if you really want to. (Do you want to?)
32. Or don't, and don't feel any shame about it. Sometimes crying takes a while. Sometimes it never comes.
33. Call the moving company.
34. Toss the toys.
35. Keep the toys, but never use them with anyone else again (and secretly smile when a friend accuses you of collecting trophies).
36. If you run into each other unexpectedly at the theater or the grocery store, nod, keep moving.
37. If you run into each other unexpectedly at the theater or the grocery store, pretend you didn't see her.
38. If you run into each other unexpectedly at the theater or the

grocery store, ask her about her life without you. Be attentive and sincere.

39. Be overcome.
40. Agree that she can keep the cats.
41. Threaten to sue her if she even thinks about taking the cats.
42. Agree to let the cats stay with her for three months and then with you for three months, on and on, until they die, one from respiratory failure, the other of loneliness.
43. Say, "Something wasn't right, I can't explain it."
44. Say, "You were the love of my life."
45. Say, "It was fun, wasn't it?"
46. Eat way too much.
47. Drink yourself silly.
48. Swear you will never love again.
49. Love again.
50. Love again immediately.

# How Not to Fall for a Lesbian Celebrity

## Joy Parks

Whether you are a seasoned lesbian or a nouveau sapphist, chances are high that, at some point, you will find yourself in the presence of an actual lesbian celebrity.

This is because, despite what both the radical Christian right and political buttons from the 1970s may tell you, lesbians do not number all that highly among the general population, and no, they are not everywhere.

Lesbians are, in fact, a rather small, clannish group that tends to congregate within a relatively limited range of locations, which explains why it is far too easy to sleep your way through the tribadist population of a small city in no time flat.

These factors—combined with an uncommonly large percentage of lesbians who pursue careers in literature, music, art, or professional sports—mean the odds are good that you will find yourself in the presence—or possibly the guest bathroom—of a genuine living legend. As a lesbian, and lacking any natural resistance to temptation, you are hereby advised how to avoid and/or deal with this unfortunate situation when it occurs.

### Avoiding the Lesbian Celebrity

In this situation, the ounce of prevention truly is not only equal to a pound of cure, it will also help you steer clear of the unpleasant circumstance of having to listen to your friends tell you that they did, indeed, tell you so.

The most effective way for you to not fall for a lesbian celebrity is to make a concerted effort not to meet one. To accomplish this goal, you must avoid the places in which they congregate. While not all the lesbians you risk meeting in these locations will be celebrities, you can never be too careful.

Generally speaking, you are best to shun fund-raising dances for good causes, music festivals, jewelry shops that favor pieces made of large abstract chunks of silver, and Walt Disney World, especially on school holidays. It will also be necessary to severely curtail visits to bookstores, particularly those not associated with the larger chains. This goes doubly for book launches, poetry readings, and independent movie screenings. You must avoid them at all costs.

Geographically, you are best to refrain from traveling in a number of highly suspect areas of the country. Avoid California, Oregon, and Vermont in their entirety; the state of Michigan mostly in August; and the eastern cape of Massachusetts in the later summer and parts of the fall. Madison, Wisconsin, no longer exists for you.

Additional ways of reducing your risk factor include avoiding all organic food establishments, vegetarian and/or vegan restaurants, and entertainment venues frequented by girl softball players.

Note that even if you have faithfully remained miles away from any and all of the locations listed above, and you still find yourself within polite conversational distance of a lesbian celebrity, you must at all times remain calm and avoid both small talk and deeper discussions. In particular, any verbal exchange must not contain the following: "While you were reading from your book/singing your song/setting the stage on fire while tap dancing your performance poem, I felt as if you uncovered my soul. That you were speaking just to me." First of all, realistically this would be impossible because the lesbian celebrity does not know you. Furthermore, it is dangerous because she may actually come to believe that she actually was singing/reading/tap dancing/soul uncovering just for you. For a little while, anyway.

*If You Do Fall for a Lesbian Celebrity*
Despite taking all of the precautions listed here, if you do find your-self in the position of having fallen for a lesbian celebrity (or having been fallen for *by* a lesbian celebrity), do not panic. There are a number of ways to mitigate any potential damage. You can also take heart in the fact that the relationship probably won't last sufficiently long for you to develop any long-term side effects or scars.

However, at this confusing and trying time in your life, you would do well to abide by the following guidelines:

Tell no one anything … so nothing comes back to haunt you.

Resist the urge to write things down. A hastily sketched note, complete with bad grammar, could quite possibly end up as a voice-over segment in someone's independent film. On the other hand, you might want to take good notes. There may be a book in this for you.

Remember that while you may be an important person in your own right, you are not as important as she is to a very large number of people. Remember this when you call her friends, concerned that she has locked herself in her office/studio/car for the last seventy-two hours and is threatening bodily harm to herself or anyone who tries to remove her. Chances are they will ask you what you did to provoke the situation.

Always pay for everything. Including your moving expenses. Both ways. You will be considered a gold digger even if your beloved is a poverty-stricken but really famous poet. So don't make it easy for them. Carry cash.

You must save everything. The brevity of the relationship shouldn't tax the average apartment's storage facilities. If she's really famous, grab a few personal items of hers on the way out the door. You deserve a nice summer house, too.

*Breaking up with a Lesbian Celebrity*

You will be amazed at how easy it is to break up with a lesbian celebrity. You need do absolutely nothing but show up. She will be breaking up with you. Don't take it personally. It's just that celebrities have more options than the rest of us, and she will be exercising hers.

You must always keep in mind that imaginative people make the best liars, and you should point out any omissions of truth as you find them. Remember that you are not the sacrifice she has to make, that she really doesn't want to give you a normal life (because then she'd be forced to live one), and no, she didn't warn you.

Do not expect to be elevated to art in her next book, song, or movie. Chances are if you do happen to be portrayed in her work, you're not going to find it flattering. In fact, you may wish to avoid the rush and retain a lawyer immediately.

On no uncertain terms following the breakup should you enter the same profession or one even vaguely related to your famous ex's. If you make a success of it (and you no doubt will, now that you actually have something to say that people want to know about), no one will ever believe that you made it on your own merits. This mistrust will be compounded if your ex's Rolodex/address book/PDA went missing for even the briefest period of time during the relationship.

And finally, remember that you are not alone. The people who got extremely weary of listening to how cool and down-to-earth she was while you were together will never tire of hearing about her uncertain hygiene, bad table manners, money problems, or lack of skill in bed.

Finding Yourself, Queerly

# How to Choose a Cock

Terry Goldie

Fourteen inches uncut. Call Fred.

If "fourteen inches uncut" means nothing to you, then you can skip this bit of self-help advice. If, on the other hand—and yes, the double entendre is going to come up constantly—there it is again—that brief phrase starts visions dancing in your brain, you are reading the right essay.

The gay male fascination with the penis fascinates me. Why are we so obsessed? There is no doubt a practical interest. It is the tool for the job. Still, heterosexual women seem to function without worrying too much about it. They learn how to play with it to the satisfaction of their partners but not much more. If they act as though they are interested in it for itself, they are usually putting on a performance for the benefit of the male behind it.

Some elements of this paean to the penis are self-plagiarized from a chapter entitled "Penis Envy" in my book *queersexlife*. That might seem inevitable, given the size of the topic, but others have written entire books on the little fellow. What they usually have not written—and I didn't either—is the most essential part: selection and maintenance.

The aforementioned straight girl usually selects a cock in the wrong order. She finds a man and then accepts whatever is hanging off him. The possible jokes are endless: the horse before the cock, any Tom's dick that's hairy, etc. To the gay man, this is impossibly misguided. The straight girl thinks that she should choose a partner who is caring, has nice eyes, will be a good father to her children. But what about what is important?

I had a dream last night. I know that is a literary device, but in this case it is just the truth. If you are a gay man you have had a version of this one. I have this straight friend. He is a card-carrying nice guy, and I have always liked him. He has a lot of success with the ladies, though I have never thought of him as a hottie. I have never seen him with his clothes off. Last night we had sex, at least in my dream.

But it was so small and so soft. I worked it over until my mouth was exhausted, with very little success. I have no idea how long the process went on, but it seemed a lifetime—and it still wasn't long.

The straight girl would have accepted that a fine catch happened to have a low-test lure. The gay man knows differently. A female friend of mine who was a sex worker had a client who was short and out of shape, with a rather ugly face, but he was hung like a horse. As she said to me, "I felt like saying to him, 'Go gay!' I knew he would never have to pay for it again."

But to go back to my title, how can we tell? I once encountered the equivalent of that client in the baths. A rather ugly man stood there smiling and then pulled back his towel to show why he was beautiful. In a place like the baths, this can work as there is space to advertise the product, but in a bar or, even worse, on the street, it can be difficult to tell. When the jeans get tighter, as they do from time to time, there is room for a reasonable guess.

You might look at the length of the fingers, the length of the feet, or the length of the nose, but the correlation is more proverbial than actual. And what if you want more—or less—than length? My favorite was a cock that was not overly large, but had a delightful smoothness and an almost conical shape. It entered any orifice smoothly and deliciously.

Of course, many assume that cocks reflect the race of the owner. This is a particular belief of size queens. I have viewed cocks of many colors, and my advice to you is that racial assumptions are likely to lead to disappointment.

Given the number of possible perversions we pursue, you might have a desire for still more complicated implements. It isn't difficult to find a pierced cock, because anyone who has one talks about it. Then again, it can be hard to find a hard one. They will tell you that piercing has no effect on tumescence, but in my limited experience, it is ... a limited experience.

What about those strange gifts of nature? Gay naturists seem to have an unusual collection of genitalia, including some that look like mariners' knots (hello, sailor?).They might attract collectors, but for practical purposes they look less than useful. Like any teacher of life skills, my question is: but what are you going to do with it?

Which takes us back to the baths. In the same way that you should test drive a car before you buy it, the cock is best chosen in a place where you can take it down the highway before things get complicated. If the straight girl used to seek a ring before taking the relationship too seriously, the gay man should try fellating the member a few times before paying too much attention to the operator.

But at the end of the day, fellatio has to lead to something beyond. In other words, if you become attached to the attachment, you are likely to become attached to the person to whom it is attached. And that can result in all kinds of trouble. One answer, of course, is to perform sort of a reverse amputation and never go beyond the root. Then again, gay men do have this horrible tendency to believe themselves to be something more than just fuckers and fuckees. But this leads to maintenance. Maintaining an erection is not easy, for either the fucker or the fuckee, especially once the cock is no longer new. As for maintaining a relationship ...

# Someday Your Prince May Come
## … Not That You'll Listen to Me

Greg Herren

Dear Young Man:

I want to tell you how happy it generally makes me to see you and your friends out in the clubs. While I realize that there are many of my peers who look at you and become enraptured by the beauty of your youth—the smooth soft skin, the full head of hair, the aura of energy—I look at you and think, "There is the future of the community." I look at your face in its innocence and wonder what the future holds for you. There are no lines on your face, no bags under your eyes; your laughter is a joy to hear. But I know that there is pain in your future—no life is free from it. My heart aches because I know you are bound to endure suffering, and I wish that I could somehow shield you from it. As I stand watching, I feel an incredible urge to help you learn from my experiences, so that you might avoid the mistakes I made.

And then I remember my own self at your age, and how little I listened to the voices of experience that tried to teach me about life. So I remain silent, because I have learned that experience is the best teacher. Life is going to throw a great many tests at you—of your character, of who you are as a person—but each of those tests carries a lesson with it. How you choose to apply that lesson to your life and behavior is the most important thing. It is incredibly easy to experience pain and become embittered and closed off. It is far harder to learn from the pain, to remain open and optimistic.

Life is what you make of it. If you see the world as a cold and dark place, that is what it will be for you. If you simply let life happen, you are wasting an incredible gift. Isn't it better to follow your dreams and try to make them happen, rather than passively waiting for them to come to you?

Everyone wants to love and to be loved. But *what* love is, is never really defined; it's always left as an abstract concept because what it is to one person is not what it is to another. You can never really know what love is until you have truly experienced it, but it is far easier to know what it is not. It isn't how it is portrayed in most movies. We all want to see the happy ending; we want the ugly duckling to turn into a swan and find happiness; we want the couple to work through their misunderstandings and live happily ever after. But life doesn't work that way; there are infinite challenges still to come even after you find love with another person. And again, it is how you handle those situations that will define you and your relationship.

On reality dating shows on TV or online hook-up/dating sites, the person looking for love has a set standard for what they are seeking—you must be this and that, you cannot be this or that. This always makes me smile, because the only common denominator in all of your failed relationships is you. There is no one perfect person out there who is everything you want. That's a fantasy, and chasing a fantasy will most likely doom you to a life alone.

For years, I believed that only by finding someone to share my life with could I fill the emptiness I felt. When I was in my early thirties, after numerous failed relationships, I took responsibility for the failures and stopped blaming the others. I didn't know what I wanted—and obviously, I was not anyone else's Mr Right, either. I came to the conclusion that I was destined to live the rest of my life alone. But rather than being depressed by the prospect, I decided to make the most of the situation. If I was going to be alone, I would be damned if I was going to be miserable. All the things I'd been putting off because I wanted to do them with my partner I started doing on my own. I joined a gym and began to work out regularly. I traveled and had adventures. I worked on myself, determined to be the best person that I could be. I stopped becoming involved in other people's dramas.

The odd thing was that my new attitude made me more appealing to others. The changes in my body from working out regularly made me more desirable. The lack of interest in finding a boyfriend freed me from the search, and I started enjoying my life much more. I saw every new man as a potential friend rather than a potential lover; this opened my life to men who enriched me. I became a better friend and started making the kinds of friends I'd always dreamed of having. I let go of the bitterness and regret—and in doing so was able to realize how good my life actually was. It was then that I found my true mate. I seriously doubt that I was ready for a relationship before I worked on myself. When I was ready, he came along. We've now been together for thirteen years.

When it comes to matters of the heart—love, desire, friendship—perhaps the most important lesson I can pass along to you is that whatever pain might arise from those intense emotions, it is neither the end of the world nor of your life. No one dies from the betrayal of a loved one, no matter how intense or exquisite the suffering.

Don't make the mistake of focusing on the negative in your life—there will always be more negativity to come. We all have a tendency to let the negative eclipse the positive, but a positive attitude and outlook will draw people to you.

Decide for yourself what you want, and figure out how you can achieve that. This lesson holds true for everything, not just relationships. Don't be afraid to chase your dreams out of a fear that you won't achieve them. The worst fate I can imagine is to look back over your life with regret. I have none about my own life. Even the bitter experiences, no matter how painful they were, were worth it—because those experiences, those bad decisions and choices that I made in my youthful ignorance, put my feet firmly on the path that led me to where I am today—and I wouldn't trade my life for anything. I learned from my experiences, and stopped making the same mistakes; by evaluating myself, I was able to move forward with a positive attitude and get to where I wanted to be.

Your prince may never come. Platitudes such as "there's someone for everyone" may not always hold true. That is why you have to make your own happiness, make a life for yourself that you are satisfied with and can enjoy. And if you do that, if and when your prince comes along, he'll see a whole person who is happy and full of joy, who loves life and squeezes everything out of it that he can—and who wouldn't want to be a part of that?

When you are young, every heartbreak seems like the end of the world. It isn't, no matter how much drama potential the heartbreak carries with it. Don't become one of those people for whom the drama becomes the most important thing. That can quickly become tiresome and will chase people away. Nothing bores me faster than people who repeat the same mistakes over and over, and will not listen, will not make the necessary changes to ensure that it never happens again. Life hands you enough real drama without having to create it for attention from your friends.

I doubt that you will listen to any of this; as I said before, I didn't listen to my elders who tried to warn me when I was your age. But even if just some of what I have said has awakened a bit of consciousness and awareness in your mind, then I have accomplished something.

I wish you well. I wish you your prince.

Sincerely,
    Greg

# Family Family (This One's for the Kids)

## Arden Eli Hill

You came out as a dyke in the fifth grade. You came out as gay to evangelical parents. You came out as trans to lesbian separatist moms. You came out as bi with no money in your savings account. You found out about the surgery that you were too young to remember, the one that caused that scar tissue, the distance between you and yourself. You came out as queer, or maybe you didn't. Maybe you just had a dick and loved dolls or had a cunt and kept your hair cut short. You came out on the streets, in the foster care system, on the couches of friends, or in the beds of older lovers. It was hard to be queer when I was young. And it is hard for you now, queer child. The movement is still chanting, "Come out, come out, wherever you are!" without opening its doors to those of you who got kicked out when you did.

Blood is thicker than water, but water will quench your thirst. I was not there the day you were born. This does not mean we cannot be family. My own parents were not there when I was born, either. They picked me up from the hospital when I was three days old, the blanket pink and tight around my body. The day you and I meet, you will be old enough to speak. When you speak, I will listen. I do not know your name, and may not know it for years, but what I do know is that we are family (queer), and I want you to be family (kin), as well.

My mother named me after her childhood doll, but even before I transitioned I was not the daughter she wanted. When I told her that I want to be a dad some day, she tried to impregnate my dream with her dramatic vengeance. Shakespeare's King Lear urged nature to curse his displeasing daughter, "If she must teem, / Create her a child of spleen, that it may live, / And be a thwart disnatur'd torment to her." My mother's face became a storm as she similarly spat out what my friends and I termed the so-called curse of the pretty, pretty princes: "May you have a child who is not like you. May you have a child who loves pink and wants to be pretty, a child who does ballet and enjoys shopping." She folded her arms across her chest and waited for me to respond. "Fine," I said, knowing that she spoke of a potential daughter. "I'll still love my son just as much."

Whether boy or girl, both or neither, the curse is impotent, because I want to encourage you to immerse yourself in what you love. Child, in my house, there will be nothing your gender or your body prohibit you from playing with. I will not try to make your interests conform or conflict with society's ideas of what you should love. I want to provide a refuge for you to be yourself and not what I was as a child or what your first family wanted you to be. I look at my friends who are femme, intersexed, boi, female, fag, gender interesting, MtF, bi-gendered, bear, or pansexual-identified, and imagine them as kids. I wish that they could have had family members that they trusted with their feelings.

Sometimes I find you when I am scrolling through the list of children available for adoption. Many of the high school kids in foster care have been there for years, but I read about an eleventh grader who has been in the system for only a month. Unlike most of the kids, she has a nearly flawless GPA. Favorite activities include physics club and varsity softball. I see your face in her photograph, a freckled girl with a beat-up baseball cap looking directly into the camera. You are also the little black child whose hair is shorn so short by each white foster mother that you cannot wear the old red barrette you have carried for years, even when everyone else in the house is asleep. I have heard you in the tales of group homes that punish residents for "inappropriate dress." You are in the nurse's office of your middle school, having your wounds cleaned out by a nurse who thinks you brought it on yourself by acting "like that." Maybe you are fifteen and know to name the way skin burns under clothes that feel antithetical to what is underneath the skin. Maybe you are five and trying not to act like a sissy or tomboy and failing. There are those of us who are known by others before we know ourselves, or before we tell.

Child, I do not believe that you are more deserving of a home because you are queer, but I do believe you are less likely to find one when who you are is not even seen as neutral but negative. I am not a queer separatist, but I will ask for you, for the queer ones and the ones who people assume are queer. Before we meet, I wish you safety in each home you inhabit. I wish you a way back to connections of blood and early experience if those connections can nurture you.

You will not be the first kid to take shelter in my home. The first was a trans guy who wanted to graduate from high school. His parents never officially kicked him out, but their house was a far cry from a home, and he wanted a fresh start, a chance to introduce himself as Robert to teachers and other kids. He slept on the couch and did the dishes, but my girlfriend at the time would only let him stay for a month and a half. He moved into a program for queer youth and got his diploma. Now he works as a carpenter in Miami. My girlfriend and I broke up, but Robert and I keep in touch. He and I joke that the wrong person moved out of the house.

I grew up knowing I was adopted. When I got old enough to think about having a family of my own, I rebelled against the idea of adoption as a last resort and the idea of adopting an older child as salt in the wound. When you arrive, it will be after much longing, work, and excitement. I know from firsthand experience the bloodless family of parents and child, and while I can't promise you a mom or another dad in the house, I can promise you a permanent parent, me, and a pair (at least) of grandparents who are getting progressively more supportive. They have been listening to my plans for a family for years, and while they still struggle with my identity, they strive to be respectful. Recently, my mother asked how I would explain to my children that they came out of their daddy's womb. "I'm not sure whose womb they are going to come out of," I tell her.

But, here is a confession that bears my conflict: I do want to give birth. I feel the urge to conceive in my blood, even with testosterone washing around my ovaries. I feel a seed there. Sometimes I want to put my female body to use, but then I remember that I already use it. My body has born me into myself, as growing up female shaped me into a person I am happy to be, someone who is working on writing, education, therapy, and physical fitness to ensure that I will be stable enough to, at some point, nurture another human being. Sometimes this is enough, and I see each child I do not bear providing space for an existing child bearing the struggle of growing up queer.

On the other hand, a former lover of mine gave birth. He welcomed his child into the world last year and like every single parent he is both father and mother. I imagine that the relationship between him and his child is more secure than other relationships between queer parents and their children. He never had to be approved by a system that is saturated by phobias, -isms, and biases. His claim to his child is a singular one, based in both blood and law. I envy that security. I'm a genderqueer faggy vegetarian who will most likely be applying to adopt as a single dad. Even though I've worked as a nanny and childcare provider for more than a decade, I worry about how sexuality and gender might make it difficult for me to convince the state that I will be a suitable parent.

Sometimes I consider the option of blending a family through birth and adoption, although I'm not even sure if my body will be able to conceive after years of testosterone. I've conjured up fantasies of a trans sperm mother.

Maybe you, my child, will have a big or little sibling waiting with me to welcome you into an environment of shelter, stability, and unconditional love. Home should be a place where, with your family, you are safe in your identity and safe to question that identity. Child, I am waiting to welcome you home.

# Leather Queer: Learning the Ropes

## Alisa Lemberg

"You are doing this for pleasure, usually your own; if it's not fun, stop." That's the most useful piece of advice I got when I entered the BDSM scene, and it is your first lesson. Understand this: what you do is your choice; you are pursuing your own desires, acting on your fantasies.

Welcome to the big, bad world of whips and chains.

Remember this: when you are introduced to Master or Mistress Big Shot who insists that all bottoms kneel at all times, and that real tops never take their clothes off or wear white leather after Labor Day—don't listen. You have navigated your way through the heteronormative culture, found your way to the leather-covered back corner of the queer world, and this is where the fun begins. But first you have to trust yourself, trust your experience and your desires. Let Mistress Big Shot play with Real Slave. You don't need them.

But here are some things you may want to think about ...

*History:* Learn your history and respect your elders (just like your Sunday school teacher said). You may have heard of the Old Guard—leather-clad men rejecting the status quo and setting into motion a side of the sexual revolution the hippie feminists never imagined. I have a tremendous amount of respect for the Old Guard: These people had the courage and strength to create a space for me to write this letter and for you to read it. They opened the dialogue of leather sex and their sacrifices paved the way for our successes. However, I am damned glad I missed those years. The Old Guard is marked by a plethora of rules and protocols; most of the kink scenes you'll find these days are a lot more free form. And, by the way, anyone under the age of fifty claiming to be Old Guard either means they fetishize Old Guard-style protocols, or they are about to tell you how you are having the wrong kind of sex. Respecting your elders doesn't mean replicating their lives.

*Creativity:* Before you go out and buy $500 worth of leather toys, figure out what you already have. Can you think of creative uses for clothespins? Wooden spoons? You can spend hundreds of dollars on paddles, floggers, and rubber clothes, but if you're living on a college-student budget, you probably don't want to. If you are just getting into the BDSM scene, I know the toys can be tempting, but they will still be at the shop next time you come by and you might have a better idea of what you're into by then. Unless, of course, it has been your lifelong dream to be whipped by a girl with a pink bunny tail holding a bright purple whip, in which case you want to go right out and buy said tail and whip (try Coyote Whips for colorful designs).

*Community:* There are plenty of kinky people who want nothing to do with other kinky people outside their bedrooms. But if you have ever gone to a Gay Student Alliance meeting or a Gay Pride event, you've probably realized that community comes with quite a few advantages. Besides, the best place to meet kinky partners is at kink community events. I've seen kink events happen in some unlikely places (Jerusalem, anyone?) so you don't have to be in New York or San Francisco to find the kink community. Get online and Google for some groups in your area. Most will have a regular event called a "munch"—this is a casual non-play event that is open to the public, and usually held in a public space. It's a nice, low-pressure, low-commitment way to meet people in your area. One thing to remember is that these events tend to be discreet, so you might not be able to tell the leather social from the librarians' Wednesday night get-together. Email the organizer in advance and ask where the event will be and if there is someone or something you can look for.

*Patience:* After years of secret desires and angst-filled fantasies, you've finally found yourself on the dungeon doorstep. Oh, who am

I kidding? With the advent of the Internet, do they still have secrets? But in any case, you are here, and ready to explore your not-so-secret desires at your local leather community center or industrial-loft-turned-dungeon. You've read the books, you've bought the toys, and you're ready to take a stab at this whole kinky sex thing. But there is just one problem: you don't have a partner. Or maybe you're in a small conservative town, and no one invited you to the dungeon because it really is a secret. Don't give up. Getting into the kink scene can be a slow process (unless you happen to be lucky enough to live in New York or San Francisco). I started in a fairly large city, and it still took me a while to build enough trust in my community to get the coveted private party invite. Furthermore, what we do takes a certain amount of skill to do safely, and skill comes from practice. You will probably not be able to swing a whip accurately on the first try; keep trying. And if you're a bottom, this is not the part you get to skim over—I know you're eager to get out there and experience all these cool things, but take some time to figure out what you want, what you need, and, most importantly, what your limits are, and then learn to communicate all that to your partner.

I used to run a munch for my local TNG group (TNG stands for The Next Generation, an offshoot of larger BDSM organizations geared to people between eighteen and thirty-five), and one of the most frequent email queries was from a potential new member describing in detail his or her fantasy—and asking for advice on how to make it happen *right now*. The only real answer is that some things are worth the wait. Good play partners, and that one scene you've always dreamed of, are certainly worth waiting for. In the meantime, enjoy the ride—and see what you can learn.

# How to Be a Country Leather Bear

## Jeff Mann

Everyone thinks of us as a city species, we leather bears. But you know better, you small-town gay men sporting beards, body hair, and brawn, you country-dwelling devotees of BDSM and rough man-on-man sex. Perhaps you live in a rural area because you grew up there to begin with and had little desire to leave, even after you realized you were queer. Perhaps you stayed in or near your hometown to be close to family or friends. Perhaps you left the city for financial reasons, to take advantage of the lower cost of living in the provinces. Perhaps you once tasted city life and recoiled, decided that living the urban gay lifestyle wasn't worth the noise and traffic, the crowds and expense, and so returned to your roots, determined to stay. Whatever the reasons for your rustic existence, know that being a country leather bear is easier than the city-loving twink might imagine.

Yes, country folks tend more toward homophobia and conservatism than frequently liberal urbanites. Most small towns sport churches on every other corner, crammed on Sundays with frothing fundamentalists convinced that men-loving-men are satanic monsters. But you, as a leather bear, are likely to deal with such unfriendly surroundings better than many of your queer brethren. There are two reasons for this. One, the outfits of the typical leather bear are identical to those of most straight country boys. In winter, both kinds of men wear work boots, cowboy boots, thermal undershirts, sweatshirts, faded jeans, leather jackets, denim jackets, and cowboy hats. In summer, they sport baseball caps, cargo shorts, camo pants, wife-beaters, muscle shirts, tank tops, and T-shirts. (The proof of this is Larry the Cable Guy, the blue-collar comedian.

Step into any bear bar, and four-fifths of the men there will resemble him.) Thus, if you choose not to be openly gay, you're well camouflaged. If you wear the typical leather-bear ensemble, you'll look like any other redneck and will more easily be able to go about your life without having to tolerate public harassment, as many of our more effeminate compatriots must. (Here's the downside: if you, like many bears, are attracted to men who look like you, you're often going to be seething with frustrated lust, surrounded by all those sexy straight men who look like leather bears but aren't.)

The second reason why living around rural conservatives is easier for leather bears is purely physical. We're not young, slender boys weak from constant dieting. We're big—bulk being part of the definition of being a bear—and our furry faces and bodies make us look manly and menacing. The intolerant are simply less likely to pick a fight with men like us. Hit the gym, buddy. Work some heft into your chest and arms. Sport a few intimidating butch tattoos. While you're at it, boxing and the martial arts are fine hobbies to adopt.

This protective coloration said and done, I'd recommend that you come out to as many of your neighbors as possible, unless they're obviously pious swine, gun collectors, or twice your size. People need to know that queers are all around them and that we come in many sizes and shapes. Diffusing ignorance diffuses hatred. Plus, it's simply easier to be honest about who you are.

So, made relatively safe by your brawn and your apparent similarity to other rural men, what you must figure out is how to lead a fulfilling life so far from Queer Central. Since you live in the countryside or a small town, spend some time exploring what pleasures these settings provide. Visit the local restaurant, doing your best to ignore the Jesus paraphernalia on the wall, and take advantage of down-home cooking at low prices that would cause city folk to faint with disbelief. Respond in kind to the servers' small-town friendliness and good country manners. Order sausage, biscuits, grits, soup, beans, chicken and dumplings, sweet iced tea, coconut cream pie. Attend seasonal celebrations that occur in your neck of the woods: the county fair, the Maple Syrup Festival, Railroad Days. For God's sake, get outdoors as often as possible. Take advantage of the natural world that city and suburban dwellers rarely get to appreciate save on vacation. Hike up to Dragon's Tooth Knob, bike the New River Trail, walk along Claytor Lake. On weekends, visit nearby state parks and national forests. Keep an eye out for hawks, butterflies, muskrats, white-tailed deer. Luxuriate in the silence, the dark country nights that city folks are denied. If you have the land, grow a garden. Pick fresh tomatoes, peppers, corn, basil, oregano, mint.

Many urban queers hanker after occasional escapes from metropolitan ruckus. Fulfilling this need is a fine way to enjoy small-town living and queer companionship at the same time. All you need is a guest room ... and a talent for cooking. Learn to mix drinks, make pasta, cook up stews, bake biscuits and pies. You're a bear, after all: you love to eat and drink. Your gay and lesbian friends eager for a change of pace from DC, San Francisco, and New York City will be grateful for a weekend in the country: quiet evenings by the fireplace, playing some guitar, sipping some bourbon, savoring some chili and cornbread, watching *Sordid Lives, Gladiator, 300,* or *The Birdcage* for the tenth time.

Country living's easier if you're resourceful and self-reliant, if you savor solitude and learn to take pleasure in small things: the shifting seasons, the changes in weather, big meals, good books, music, and movies. The frost on the windowpane resembles feathers. There's a new cheese at the local Food City, a new variety of Scotch at the liquor store. Joni Mitchell just released a new CD. The latest Netflix DVD has Viggo Mortensen naked. The sexily goateed FedEx man just delivered, unbeknownst to him, porno star François Sagat bound and gagged in the latest Titan video release *Fear.*

Come to terms with country masculinity and winnow it; take the best and throw away the rest. Many of us, once we discovered our homosexuality, rejected traditional masculine activities, the ones so beloved of small-town folks dedicated to old-fashioned gender roles. Look again. You can be brave *and* nurturing, strong *and* tender. Many apparently mutually exclusive things are really not. Honor, loyalty, stoicism, and protectiveness are warrior virtues more than worth retaining. As besieged as the queer community is these days, we need all the warriors (male and female) we can get.

Many of us, influenced by media and the prevailing urban values of the queer community, tend to hold country enthusiasms in contempt. Look again. Pickup trucks are handy as hell, and damned handsome at that. Whether live or televised, basketball, football, and baseball games can be pretty pleasurable. The players are often sexy, the beer and hot dogs cheap and tasty. Country music brims with top-notch guitar playing and heartfelt lyrics. Along with Reba McEntire, Dolly Parton, and other country divas so adored by drag queens, there's a passel of fuckable and furry studs who apotheosize the concept of Sexy Country Boy, prominent among them lean and furry otter Tim McGraw, hunky goateed Chris Cagle, burly blond bear Toby Keith, and adorable cublet Chris Young—all ripe subjects for kidnapping fantasies and fodder for erotic fiction.

In other words, you don't need to be the sleek, smooth, slender, well-groomed, androgynous, and thoroughly domesticated city queer of many an *Advocate* ad or TLA movie. You can preserve a little wildness, like the rural landscape around you. You can be as beefy and scruffy as many a country boy and still be thoroughly queer.

Adding gay erotic elements to a country life can be challenging, but between the Internet and an active imagination, you can work wonders. Try to picture what being a country queer of any stripe was like before web browsing! It was an isolation that bred soul-killing loneliness, despair, and suicidal thoughts. Now a few minutes on Firefox can net you a slew of distant delights. Order BDSM gear—bondage tape, handcuffs, ball gags, hoods, tit clamps, and other toys beloved of leather bears—from faraway stores such as Mr. S (*mr-s-leather.com*) or JT's Stockroom (*male.stockroom.com*). Buy erotic bondage art from countries as remote as Japan. (Check out the amazing work of Gengoroh Tagame for evocative, arousing images of muscle bears bound, gagged, tortured, and raped.) For a small membership fee, drool over roped-up studs on sites like *bearbound.com*. And if you're single or in an open relationship, hunt down partners for long-distance flirtation. Check out *worldleathermen.com*, *bear411.com*, or *musclebear.com* to chat with men who share your physique and erotic interests. If you're lucky, you might even lure one into visiting. Back to that guest bedroom and that cookbook collection. There are lots of city-pent leather boys likely to relish a cozy weekend in your B&D B&B, bound to your bed or treated to your home cooking.

If you affix a leather- or bear-flag sticker to the back window of your pickup truck, you might meet friends or playmates even closer to home. A note with a stranger's phone number or email address might be waiting for you beneath your windshield wiper when you're done fetching groceries and cruising the sexy young clerk at Food City. And being out to your neighbors is likely to net you advice regarding the location of local queers. Sociable small-town folks are often eager to introduce people with similar interests.

It takes imagination to infuse daily life—which tends toward the habitual, the boring, and the mundane—with erotic energy, whether you're partnered or single. It's even harder in the queer-sparse countryside, but, if achieved, it adds an edge and intensity that we leather bears cherish. Wear that chain-and-padlock slave collar beneath your sweater when you go to work, or the naughty BUTCH BEAR: HAIRY, HORNY, HUNGRY T-shirt you bought online. Slip in a butt plug for your workout at the local YMCA. Take pleasure in the weight of a chrome doughnut cock ring while attending the baseball game. Handcuff and bit-gag your partner before cuddling on the couch to watch the latest Netflix delivery. Leave him hogtied and ball-gagged on the floor of the closet for an hour on Sunday morning, while the rest of the county sings hymns in church. Half of the pleasure of being a kink-buff living in a rural/conservative area is knowing how much you're getting away with and picturing the expressions on your neighbors' faces if they only knew.

Finally, save the money and take the time to travel, whether it's to the nearest small city for a bear- or leather-run, to San Francisco to check out the infamous bear bar the Lone Star, to DC to admire all the bare and hairy torsos during Green Lantern's Shirtless Night, to Key West for the clothing-optional, all-male guesthouses, or overseas to explore the leather bars of Vienna, London, and Berlin. Novelty is exhilarating, you'll see what you're missing, you'll admire the plethora of sexy city men, if you're lucky you'll bind, gag, and bed a few, and you'll ravish a few restaurants too. Then you'll be ready to go home, where there are still trees and pastures, where things are slow enough for folk culture, tradition, and good manners to survive, where the nights are very dark, and you can see the stars.

# How to Be a Visible Femme

## Stacia Seaman

You sit there in the coffee shop, your hair hanging down your back. With a graceful gesture, you tuck a strand behind your ear and then turn the page of your book. You take a sip of your latte and put down the mug, a plum-colored kiss barely visible on the rim. In your casual outfit, you are young and beautiful. A graduate student, perhaps. A new bride. A mother celebrating her freedom now that her child is in daycare. And that's the problem.

"Nobody knows I'm gay," you say. "They take one look at me and assume I'm straight. They ask me what I'm doing in 'their' bars. They tell me to go back to my boyfriend. They tell me they don't want to be my 'experiment.'"

Maybe, you think, if you cut your hair short. If you wore less feminine clothing. If you stopped wearing makeup. Maybe if you tried to look more like a lesbian, you'd be more accepted in the lesbian community. You wouldn't be invisible.

Thing is, you wouldn't be you.

But are you really invisible?

Now that I look more carefully, I recognize the title of the book you're reading. I see the rainbow colors of your keychain. There's a quiet confidence about you. You don't question who you are—what you are—and you don't hide it, either.

You are femme.

When you walk into a club by yourself, to most of the women, you are nobody. The looks you get are scornful, disdainful. "We're not here for your boyfriend's enjoyment," they say. "We're not interested in 'bi until graduation.' We only date real lesbians."

But put you on the arm of a butch, of a tomboi, and everything changes. You can feel the appraising glances. You know you're being cruised. You're a real lesbian. Desirable.

It's not fair, you think. Why do so many lesbians only see you when you're part of a couple? You don't define yourself in terms of who you're with. And why should you? You have a strong sense of self, of identity. You don't need to be validated. But you need to be recognized. You need to be seen. To be visible.

Ask yourself this: who do you want to see you?

When you wear your skirts, your shoes, your sexy lingerie; when you put on your perfume, your makeup; when you brush your hair until it shines—when you do all of this, it's not to fit in. It's not to look straight or to make your life easier.

You're doing it for yourself, yes, because this is who you are, but you're also doing it for them.

For the butches.

You know it, and they know it.

So why can't they see you?

Well, I'll tell you. Come a little closer.

*Butches can be a bit dense.*

It's really just that simple. If they don't see you, it's because you need to make yourself seen. And that's not to say you should get a mullet and wave a rainbow flag. It's all about a way of walking. A come-hither look in your eyes. A secret smile.

You need to make the butches' knees melt.

You've got the power here. Use it.

You know what you want. That gorgeous butch by the pool table. The one with the tank top, the jeans with the faded outline of a wallet in the back pocket, the black Harley boots. She's drinking beer out of the bottle while she waits for her turn. You love the way her muscles flex when she lifts it to her lips. You love her confident swagger when she approaches her shot.

You want to see that confident swagger when she approaches *you*. You want her to see you. You want her to want you.

So here's what you have to do. You have to look her in the eye with that look that says, "I want you." Don't try to hide your admiration. Let it shine through.

She's butch. She'll know what that look means. She's not going to worry about a nonexistent boyfriend; she knows exactly what you like.

That might not be enough, though. She might need a little more encouragement. She knows what you like—butches—but she might be shy, or she might be clueless. So talk to her. Ask her to dance. And when you get to the dance floor, let her lead. After all, she is the butch. Remember, you have to make the first move in a way that makes her think *she's* making the move.

It might not work the first time. Or the second. Or even the third. The individual chemistry might not be there, or the woman you approach might already have a partner. But no butch is going to be offended by the attentions of a femme.

For everything you love about butches—the faint scent of motor oil, the strength of their hands, the way they hold the door for you—they love something about *you*. Yes, a butch is looking for the packaging: the clothes, the hair, the makeup. But the butch is also looking for the intangibles: the attitude, the energy, the confidence of the femme.

She wants her knees to go weak as much as you do. So make them.

You don't have to say a word. Use your power. Give her that look. Give her that smile. The one that says you know what you are, you know what you want, and it's her.

She'll recognize it.

She'll respond. Even if it's just with a shy smile and a blush she tries to hide by ducking her head.

As for the rest of them—do you really care? You are who you are, and you know what you want, and if they don't or won't see that, does that take away from who you are? The reality is, some women will still look at you the way they always have. They'll accuse you of trying to pass, of taking the easy way out. And you know what? That's fine. Let them believe what they want to believe. Don't try to change for them. It won't work. Besides, they're not the ones you're concerned with.

Instead, be who you are. Keep wearing your skirts. Keep styling your hair. And keep smiling that secret smile, knowing that butches everywhere see you. You're visible.

# Bottoms Up

## Clarence Wong

You're convinced it's your carefully tended five o'clock shadow. That and your buzz cut, so reminiscent of David Beckham in the Armani underwear ad. Those are what are attracting the sexy young man to you.

He stations himself across from you in the dim hallway of the bathhouse. Leaning the back of his head against the wall, he stands with his legs confidently apart. He is gloriously naked except for a slender leather harness slung across his chest. The polished metal studs of the harness glint softly in the half-light. The young man fixes his gaze directly at you, the boldest and most unequivocal signal of desire you've received all night.

Despite the immediate stirring under the towel draped around your hips, you hesitate. You're not accustomed to being cruised by a sexy young man. You're used to being cruised by older men, men with thinning hair, thick moustaches, beer guts, and rough hands. You could always count on turning their heads as you sauntered around the bathhouse, basking in your youth.

But times have changed. With age, your once slender frame has thickened with muscle and flesh. The older men don't look hungrily your way anymore. A new age calls for a new look, you decide. A new look and a fresh strategy of sexual attraction. You embark on a makeover. Your once tumbling, wavy hair is now shorn to military neatness. Your once smooth face now bristles with daredevil stubble. You lift weights with new vigor so that your muscle mass compensates for the growing layers of flesh encasing your body. You sweat and grunt and push and pull in the hope your new look will bring forth a fresh crop of sexual possibilities.

The young man's gaze is strong and unwavering. His hand slides down and he strokes himself enticingly, the universal come-hither signal of bathhouses everywhere. Even as you step across the hallway toward him, you wonder if you're up for this fresh challenge. You have no experience with a sexy young man. Will you live up to his expectations? Will you know how to lift him up to the pinnacles of excitement and passion? He is seeking a competent top, you are certain, but you have neither the confidence nor the backing of experience that you are that top.

With respect to the ever-important top-bottom question, you consider yourself "versatile." At least, that's how you list yourself in your online cruising profile. You're not sure what that really means, but since more than half of the online cruisers list themselves as versatile, you figure that is a safe choice.

You suspect you're probably not authentically versatile. Versatile implies *both* top and bottom—sometimes the one, sometimes the other—whereas you're probably more *neither* than *both*. Neither pounding someone's ass, nor being pounded, particularly appeals to you. Other than ass pounding, your idea of heaven encompasses pretty much every erotic act in the sexual lexicon—cock and balls play, dirty kissing, rimming, erotic touching, exhibitionism, threeways, and more. You are truly versatile, but you know that's not what gay men mean when they say "versatile."

The young man's face is handsome. Blond hair parted at the side, deep-set eyes, a rakish moustache over his upper lip. His body is smooth, shaved to the very last pubic hair. You caress his shoulders slowly, his chest, his abdomen. Closing his eyes, the young man throws his head back, relishing the sensation of your palms and fingers. He pulls your face down to his nipple. It is turgid and expectant. You flick your tongue and he moans.

You reach behind the young man. His buttocks, full and firm like foam pillows, yield to the squeeze of your hands. He moves his hips in a way that clearly tells you what he wants. Pulling his cheeks apart, your fingers probe his crack. You discover it is already greased. With your middle finger, you rub the entrance in a circular motion, and then your finger slips easily into his hole.

The young man sighs. "Oh man, that feels good. Go for it, I'm completely clean down there," he confidently assures you.

Sucking and occasionally biting his nipple, you penetrate him: first one, then two, then three fingers are inserted into his crack. The young man brushes his lips over your ear. "Let's go to my room." You nod. He smiles and leads you down the hallway.

In his room, the young man is brisk, all business. On a ledge beside the bed, he has laid out condoms, lube, poppers, and a bottle of Evian. He stretches out on the bed and smiles at you. "What would you like to do?"

He takes your breath away, this sexy young man. He is beautiful, no doubt, but more than that, you are dazzled by his confidence and ease. He is twenty years younger than you, and yet you were never that confident at his age. You are barely that confident now.

"Your fingers in my ass, that was hot." He flips over onto his belly. His buttocks are shapely mounds of golden flesh. "Wanna fist me?"

Your eyes widen. You've always been curious to try. "I've never done that before," you say.

"Really?" he says, smiling. "I'm surprised. Here, I'll teach you." He raises his hand and gathers his fingertips together. "Make like a quacking duck."

You raise your hand and follow suit.

"That's how you enter me, at an angle."

He reaches for the bottle of lube and pours it liberally over your quacking duck fist. Twisting around, he pours more lube on his crack. "I'm ready," he says.

With furrowed brow, you place your fist next to his crack. Applying pressure, you insert the tips of your thumb and fingers into his hole.

"Slow, slow," he says, hissing with pleasure. "That feels great. Mind your fingernails."

Applying more pressure, your thumb and fingers disappear bit by bit into his hole. When your knuckles are about to be absorbed by his sphincter, you stop.

He juts his butt up higher. "Yeah, like that, just like that. This is your first time? Man, you're good. Now, slowly pull out and then plunge back in again."

Your thumb and fingers slip easily out of his crack. More confident now, you reinsert them into his hole. This time, it feels less like you're penetrating his ass and more like his ass is absorbing your fist. When your knuckles reach the entrance of his crack, you pause. Taking a deep breath, you push your fist forward. Your knuckles slip past his sphincter and enter the warm inner sanctum of his ass.

The young man groans and arches his back. "Man, that's hot. Go ahead, deeper."

You push again and your entire fist is soon buried in his ass, up to your wrist. The sensation is exquisite, like a tight, close embrace.

"Look at that," he says, turning to the mirrored wall next to the bed. "Fucking hot." You turn to the mirror and see the two of you, naked and aroused. You see the young man's smooth body stretched out on the bed, his ass in the air. You see yourself sitting next to him on the edge of the narrow bed, your fist buried in his ass, your arm extending out of his ass. The two of you are one contiguous being.

"You're hard," says the young man, smiling. You look in the mirror to see your flaming erection.

"I want to suck you," he says. "Let's switch places. I'll get up and you lie down, but keep your fist in my ass."

You're not exactly sure how the two of you manage it, but somehow, like acrobats in a Cirque du Soleil extravaganza, you switch places with the young man so that now you are stretched out on the bed while he stands beside you. Throughout this maneuver, your fist remains buried in his ass.

He bends down and goes to work on your boner. It doesn't take long. "You had a big load," he says, licking his lips. "Your cum tastes sweet."

You smile and nod your head, not trusting yourself to speak. You're still gasping from the release.

Later, in the spacious shower room of the bathhouse, the young man is relaxed, chatty. He tells you he's from Chicago, he's in town for work. His banter is light, jocular, as if you are showering after shooting a friendly game of hoops.

As the two of you are toweling dry, a man emerges from the steam room next door. He is short and stocky with muscular shoulders and biceps. The sexy young man's eyes follow him as he walks by.

"Well, see you around." The young man quickly wraps a towel around his waist and hurries out of the shower room.

Alone, you stare after the young man. Unexpectedly, fragments of a Latin benediction from Catholic school days waft into your head. The long-forgotten words are half-formed, their meaning misty, something about almighty God, creatures great and small, eternal love. And yet, despite the incomplete evocation of this distant memory, you are filled with the spirit of the benediction.

With all your heart, you bless the sexy young man. You bless his youth, his beauty, his confidence. You bless him for giving you one evening of hot sex, for fulfilling your fisting fantasy. Most of all, you bless him for teaching you that the key to being a bottom, a successful bottom, is to always be on top of your game.

# Just This Moment:
# A Letter to David Wojnarowicz

## Mattilda Bernstein Sycamore

Dear David—

I found you in an obituary. Or it wasn't exactly an obituary, but an article that appeared right after you died and *Memories That Smell Like Gasoline* came out, and I read that article and thought: Oh. Then I picked up the book and saw your drawings of sex so alienated and intimate, infinite and lost, I wasn't prepared for what I recognized: "When I was nine or ten some guy picked me up in Central Park + took me home. He made a polaroid of me sitting in a chair. It didn't show my face so I let him keep it."

So right then I read *Close to the Knives* instead: it was the first time I found my rage in print, and simultaneously a feeling of maybe a little bit of hope in a world of loss. I recognized so much in your words and images and their textures, I couldn't hold you, but I held your rage. I held your desperation and it helped me to feel. Everything.

You wrote about a "disease in the American landscape," the literal disease of AIDS, but a crisis caused because the people in power decided who was expendable, and queers and drug addicts and poor people and people of color were left to die. You're so intent on exposing the layers of oppression between government and God and family and the "one tribe nation" of "walking swastikas." One minute you're driving through the landscape of light and dark, shadow and memory and space so much space and all of a sudden: "I feel that I'm caught in the invisible arms of government in a country slowly dying beyond our grasp."

You wrote mostly from downtown New York in the 1980s, but here in San Francisco in the early 1990s right after you died we felt that too. The people I met, we knew it was the beginning of the end, but still it was the beginning. Most of us had recently escaped our families of origin, we were scarred and broken and brutalized but determined to create something else, something we could live with, something we could call home or healing or even just help, I need help here—can you help? We were incest survivors, whores, outcast kids, vegans, anarchists, runaways, and addicts trying not to disappear. We knew that the world wanted us dead, but we were ready for something else; we didn't always know what it was, but we were ready—and if we weren't ready, then we were getting ready.

This was the early 1990s in San Francisco, so everywhere people were dying of AIDS and drug addiction and suicide and some of the dead were among us, just like us, just trying to survive. Others were more in the distance, elders like you who we barely got to know except through your loss. We went crazy and cried a lot, or went crazy and stopped crying, or just went crazy.

I carried *Close to the Knives* around like a litmus test, when I met someone new I'd hand it off—some would turn to me and say oh, this is too much, I can't handle it. Others would look me in the eyes with recognition and those were the ones. You helped me to embrace my rage like a "blood-filled egg," a shift in the texture of breathing, a way to further opportunities for connection rather than just the isolation we knew so well, you and I and others like us struggling to survive.

Of course, you were already dead—even when you conjured this world of bathrooms and parks and alleys and rotting piers and other public opportunities for sexual splendor, I was "gasping from a sense of loss and desire." Sure, "I was afraid the intensity of my fantasies would become strangely audible," but I knew that this public engagement with the sexual could infuse all moments of hope and horror, escape and claustrophobia, landscape and longing, death and remembrance.

This was the Mission in the early '90s, and I was living among queer freaks and artists and activists and sluts creating defiant and desperate ways to love and lust for and take care of one another in crowded, crumbling apartments painted in garish hues and decorated with other people's trash. We paraded down the streets in bold and ragged clothes too big or too small, we shared thrift store treasures and recipes and strategies for getting day-glow hair dye to last. We exchanged manifestos and zines and fliers and gossip, got in dramatic fights over politics, over the weather, over clothing, over who was sleeping with whom; we held each other, we painted each other's nails and broke down, honey we broke down.

You were among the heroes whose books my friends and I exchanged at lightning speed—Dorothy Allison and Cherrie Moraga, Leslie Feinberg and Sapphire. David, I carried you around in my bag for years and sometimes when anything or everything was too much I would just hold you: I was learning and living and giving the potential of embracing outsider status in order to create safety, love, community, desire, home on my own terms. And you reinforced this drive to build my own systems for understanding and challenging the world, my own sense of morality. You knew that "Hell is a place on earth. Heaven is a place in your head." Queerness became "a wedge that I might successfully drive between me and a world that was rapidly becoming more and more insane."

My friends and I were huddled and dreaming outside of the status quo, but still we were gentrifiers—we knew that. Some of us had grown up rich and more of us poor, but we could see the way that queer freaks and artists and activists made the Mission a safer place for the yuppies we despised. We brought the trendy restaurants and boutiques that we gazed at with anguish and disgust, the partying suburbanites we scorned. We were the beginning of the end, and we didn't know what to do because we'd just found the beginning.

David, reading *Close to the Knives* again after all these years I'm struck by your sense of a shared destiny between all people with AIDS or all queers or all marginal artists, this community of desperation, and I'm struck by how this feeling of commonality is now almost entirely lost. I can't help wondering if it was ever there, if your work built such potential for delirious accountability yet also participated in a glamorization of fringe cultures, preventing a more nuanced examination of gentrification. Or maybe things have just changed so dramatically in fifteen years that there is no longer an "us." You invoke the urban imagination with such urgency and potential, yet the public sex you helped me to claim has almost disappeared from communal possibility. Still I keep searching for those moments when everything becomes lighter or brighter or easier to imagine; I wonder about these gestures of loneliness that can somehow create an expression so dense it becomes splendid: Hold me. Now.

You ask: "If we all die off what will happen to those we leave behind who are just this moment being born?" I'm still struggling to imagine.

Love—
mattilda

CONTRIBUTORS' BIOGRAPHIES

Dr Kevin Alderson is an associate professor of counseling psychology (Division of Applied Psychology, Faculty of Education) at the University of Calgary. His areas of research interest include all aspects of human sexuality, gender studies, and gay identity. Throughout his career as a psychologist, Dr Alderson has counseled hundreds of sexual minority clients, and he currently maintains a part-time private practice. Before joining the university in July 2001, he was the Head of Counselling and Health Services at Mount Royal College in Calgary. He writes a monthly column for *Gay Calgary* magazine and has published five books, including: *Beyond Coming Out: Experiences of Positive Gay Identity* (Insomniac Press, 2000); *Breaking Out: The Complete Guide to Building and Enhancing a Positive Gay Identity for Men and Women* (Insomniac Press, 2002); and *Same-Sex Marriage: The Personal and the Political*, co-authored with Dr Kathleen A. Lahey (Insomniac Press, 2004).

Mette Bach is in her final year of the Creative Writing MFA program at the University of British Columbia. She wrote the syndicated humor column, "Not That Kind of Girl," for nearly four years. Her new column, "From Queer to Eternity," appears in *Xtra! West*. She freelances for *The Advocate*, *WestEnder*, *Vancouver Review*, and *Vancouver* magazine. Her other anthologized work appears in *Visible: A Femmethology* (*femmethology.com*), *Fist of the Spider Woman* (Arsenal Pulp Press, 2009), and the Lambda Literary Award-winning anthology *First Person Queer* (Arsenal Pulp Press, 2007).

Victor J. Banis, an early rabble-rouser for gay rights and freedom of the press, is the author of more than 150 published novels and numerous shorter pieces, in a career spanning nearly half a century.

His most recent works are *Lola Dances* (MLR Press, 2008); *Deadly Nightshade* (MLR Press, 2008); and *Angel Land* (Regal Crest, 2008). A native of Ohio and longtime Californian, he lives and writes now in West Virginia's beautiful Blue Ridge and travels extensively in support of LGBT writing and causes.

**Paul Bellini** was born in Timmins, Ontario in 1959. After receiving his Bachelor of Arts in Film Studies at York University in 1982, he embarked on a career that includes being a writer on two of Canada's foremost comedy series, *The Kids in the Hall* (1989 to 1995) and *This Hour Has 22 Minutes* (1995 to 1999). Other writing assignments have included the novel *Buddy Babylon* (Dell, 1998); the theatrical presentation *The Lowest Show on Earth* (2002); and the independent films *Hayseed* (1997) and *doUlike2watch.com* (2002). He has also worked on television shows as both writer and producer, a career that has garnered three Gemini Awards and three Emmy nominations; and he has also published more than 100 articles for the Toronto-based magazine *fab*. He lives in Toronto.

**Steven Bereznai** is the author of *Gay and Single...Forever? 10 Things Every Gay Guy Looking for Love (and Not Finding It) Needs to Know* (Da Capo, 2006). His journalism includes a stint as editor-in-chief of *fab*, Toronto's gay scene magazine, articles in the *Toronto Star, NOW, Xtra!,* and *Icon*, as well as nine years at CBC Newsworld as a writer/producer.

**S. Bear Bergman** is the author of *Butch Is a Noun* (Suspect Thoughts Press, 2006) and *The Nearest Exit May Be Behind You* (forthcoming from Arsenal Pulp Press in 2009) as well as co-editor with Kate Bornstein of *Gender Outlaws: The Next Generation* (forthcoming from Seal Press, 2010). Ze has also written and continues to perform three award-winning solo works, and has contributed to numerous anthologies on a variety of topics from the sacred to the extremely profane. Bear works at the points of intersection between and among gender, sexuality, and culture (and spends a lot of time keeping people from installing traffic signals there) and lives in Burlington, Ontario, with hir fiancé, activist j wallace. *sbearbergman. com*.

**Tony Correia** writes the monthly column "Queen's Logic" for *Xtra! West* in Vancouver. His personal essays have appeared in the *Globe and Mail*, the *Vancouver Province*, and *sub-Terrain* magazine. For everything Tony Correia, visit *tonycorreia.com*.

**Daniel Allen Cox** is the author of the novel *Shuck* (Arsenal Pulp Press, 2008), the novella *Tattoo This Madness In* (Dusty Owl Press, 2006), and the story chapbook *Episodes of Deflated Magic* (Fever Press, 2004). His stories have appeared in the anthology *Year of the Thief* (Thieves Jargon Press, 2006) and in numerous magazines. He writes the column "Fingerprinted" for *Capital Xtra!*, and lives in Montreal.

**Maggie Crowley** is an artist, activist, and teacher committed to community, social change, and sequins. She is the founder and artistic director of "The Femme Show," bringing femme visibility and queer art for queer people to the masses. She has been seen with Boston's Traniwreck, as a guest artist with Body Heat: Femme Porn Tour at Dixon Place's Hot! Festival, and at the Femme2008 conference. She is a former whiz kid activist and teen prodigy poet. Info at *thefemmeshow.com*.

**Amber Dawn** is a writer, filmmaker, and performance artist based in Vancouver. She is the co-editor of *With a Rough Tongue: Femmes Write Porn* (Arsenal Pulp Press, 2006), and the editor of *Fist of the*

*Spider Woman* (Arsenal Pulp Press, 2009). Her award-winning gen-
derfuck docuporn, *Girl on Girl*, screened in eight countries and has
been added to the gender studies curriculum at Concordia University. She has toured three times with the infamous US "Sex Workers'
Art Show." She has an MFA in Creative Writing from the University
of British Columbia.

**Lewis DeSimone** is the author of the novel *Chemistry* (Lethe Press,
2008). His work has also appeared in *Christopher Street*, the *James
White Review*, the *Harrington Gay Men's Fiction Quarterly*, and
the anthologies *Beyond Definition: New Writing from Gay and
Lesbian San Francisco* (Manic D Press Inc, 1994); *Charmed Lives:
Gay Spirit in Storytelling* (White Crane Books, 2006); *Best Gay
Love Stories: Summer Flings* (Alyson Books, 2007); and *My Diva:
65 Gay Men on the Women Who Shaped Their Lives* (University
of Wisconsin Press, 2009). He blogs regularly at *SexandtheSissy.
wordpress.com*. A native Bostonian, Lewis lives in San Francisco,
where he is working on his second novel. He can be reached through
*lewisdesimone.com*.

**Viet Dinh** was born in Đà Lat, Vietnam in 1974 and spent his for-
mative years in Aurora, Colorado. He earned his MFA from the
University of Houston and lives in Wilmington, Delaware. In 2008,
he received a Fiction Fellowship from the National Endowment for
the Arts. His work has appeared in the *O. Henry Prize Stories* 2009
(Anchor, 2009), *Zoetrope: All-Story*, *Threepenny Review*, *Five
Points*, *Chicago Review*, *Fence*, *Michigan Quarterly Review*, and
*Epoch*, among others.

**Julie R. Enszer** is a poet and writer living in Maryland. She has an
MFA from the University of Maryland and is enrolled in the PhD
program in Women's Studies at the University of Maryland. Her

poems have been published in *Iris: A Journal About Women*, *Room of One's Own*, *Long Shot*, the *Harrington Park Lesbian Literary Quarterly*, *Feminist Studies*, and the *Women's Review of Books*. You can read more about her work at *julierenszer.com*.

**B.J. Epstein** is a writer, editor, and Swedish-to-English translator. She is completing her PhD in translation studies at Swansea University in Wales. For more information, see *awaywithwords.se* or *brave-new-words.blogspot.com*.

**Stacey May Fowles'** work has been published in various online and print magazines, including *Kiss Machine*, the *Absinthe Literary Review*, and *sub-Terrain*. Her nonfiction has been anthologized in the widely acclaimed *Nobody Passes: Rejecting the Rules of Gender and Conformity* (Seal Press, 2006), and in the Lambda Literary Award winner *First Person Queer* (Arsenal Pulp Press, 2007). Her first novel, *Be Good*, was published by Tightrope Books in November 2007, and in fall 2008 she released an illustrated novel, *Fear of Fighting*, from Invisible Publishing. She lives in Toronto where she is the publisher of *Shameless*, a feminist magazine for teenage girls.

**Sky Gilbert** is a writer, director, and drag queen extraordinaire. He was co-founder and artistic director of Buddies in Bad Times Theatre (North America's largest gay and lesbian theater) for eighteen years. His books include the novels *Guilty* (Insomniac Press, 1998), *St. Stephen's* (Insomniac Press, 1999) and *I Am Kasper Klotz* (ECW Press, 2001), the theater memoir *Ejaculations from the Charm Factory* (ECW Press, 2000), and two poetry collections, *Digressions of a Naked Party Girl* (ECW Press, 1998) and *Temptations for a Juvenile Delinquent* (ECW Press, 2003). He has received two Dora Mavor Moore Awards and the Pauline McGibbon Award for theater directing, and was recently the recipient of the Margo Bindhardt

Award (from the Toronto Arts Foundation), the Silver Ticket Award (from the Toronto Alliance for the Performing Arts), and the Re-Lit Award for his fourth novel, *An English Gentleman* (Cormorant Books, 2003). He also recently received a PhD from the University of Toronto. Sky had two books published in 2007: the novel *Brother Dumb* (ECW Press) and the play *Bad Acting Teachers* (Playwrights Canada Press). His most recent novel, *Wit in Love* (Quattro), was published in 2008. Sky holds a University Research Chair in Creative Writing and Theatre Studies at the School of English and Theatre Studies at the University of Guelph.

**Terry Goldie** is author of *queersexlife: Autobiographical Notes on Sexuality, Gender & Identity* (Arsenal Pulp Press, 2008); *Pink Snow: Homotextual Possibilities in Canadian Fiction* (Broadview Press, 2003); and *Fear and Temptation: The Image of the Indigene in Canadian, Australian, and New Zealand Literatures* (McGill-Queen's, 1989). He is editor of *In a Queer Country: Gay and Lesbian Studies in the Canadian Context* (Arsenal Pulp Press, 2001), and co-editor, with Daniel David Moses, of *An Anthology of Canadian Native Literature in English* (Oxford Press, 2005). His next project is tentatively titled *John Money: The Man Who Invented Gender*.

**Wes Hartley** is a queer elder. He's been out since 1966. He's been writing for more than fifty years and has completed twenty-one books. In the past, he's been a volunteer mentor to queer (and other) teens and a freelance counselor on drug issues to youths. He lives in Vancouver.

**Greg Herren** is the award-winning author of *Murder in the Rue Chartres* (Alyson Books, 2007), and co-editor of *Love, Bourbon Street: Reflections on New Orleans* (Alyson Books, 2006). A long-time activist, his day job is with the NO/AIDS Task Force, and he also serves as an at-large member of the Board of Directors of the National Stonewall Democrats. His work has appeared in *Ellery Queen's Mystery Magazine* and *New Orleans Noir* (Akashic, 2007), as well as in many other anthologies and magazines and on many websites. He lives in the shadow of a questionable levee system in New Orleans with his partner of thirteen years and a bipolar cat.

**Arden Eli Hill** is an all-around queer with an MFA in Creative Writing from Hollins University. His primary partner and genre is poetry, though he enjoys encounters with erotica, creative nonfiction, and the critical essay. Arden is a poetry editor for *Breath and Shadow*, an online journal of disability culture and literature. In 2008, he was a poetry fellow at the Lambda Literary Retreat for Emerging Writers. Arden's work has been accepted or published by *Sein und Werden, Willow Springs, Ghoti Magazine, Concrete, The Hollins Critic*, the 2008 *Windy City Times Pride Literary Supplement*, the 2007 and 2008 *Inglis House Poetry Chapbook, Breath and Shadow, Wordgathering, Best Gay Erotica* 2008, *Boys in Heat, love-youdivine.com*, and the Lambda Literary Award-winning anthology *First Person Queer* (Arsenal Pulp Press, 2007). Arden is extremely grateful for the support and encouragement of his friend Trip.

**Roz Kaveney** is a slightly over-worked critic, novelist, poet, and activist living in London.

**Sean Michael Law** lives in Denver with his partner Matt and his thirteen-year-old daughter Andy. He earned his MA in English at the University of Colorado at Boulder, and teaches at the Community Colleges of Colorado Online in the English Department. Sean has begun focusing on his writing, working on several short stories and a novel. He has been published in the United States, most recently in the *Harrington Gay Men's Literary Quarterly*. His life is a busy confluence of teachers, students, celebrities, dogs, knitting, writing, and yoga.

**Suki Lee** is the author of a collection of short stories, *Sapphic Traffic* (Conundrum Press, 2003). Her fiction has been widely published in such anthologies as *Hot & Bothered 3* (Arsenal Pulp Press, 2001) and *4* (Arsenal Pulp Press, 2003), *The Portable Conundrum* (Conundrum Press, 2006), *With a Rough Tongue: Femmes Write Porn* (Arsenal Pulp Press, 2006), and *Fist of the Spider Woman: Tales of Fear and Queer Desire* (Arsenal Pulp Press, 2009). She has an MA from Concordia University's Creative Writing and English Literature program. Suki Lee was born in Montreal and lives in Toronto. More info: *sukilee.com*.

**Alisa Lemberg** went to her first leather bar in Amsterdam and has explored kink in some unlikely places, including Asia and the Middle East. A caffeine addict with an affinity for chai, she started a social gathering called Coffee and Kink in Boston, and is currently on a pilgrimage to the queer Mecca of San Francisco. Her work also appears in *Visible Vol. 2* (Homofactus Press, 2009).

**Jeff Mann** grew up in Covington, Virginia, and Hinton, West Virginia, receiving degrees in English and forestry from West Virginia University. His poetry, fiction, and essays have appeared in many publications, including *The Spoon River Poetry Review*, *Wild Sweet Notes: Fifty Years of West Virginia Poetry 1950-1999* (Publishers Place, 2000), *Prairie Schooner*, *Shenandoah*, *Laurel Review*, the *Gay and Lesbian Review Worldwide*, *Crab Orchard Review*, *West Branch*, *Bloom*, and *Appalachian Heritage*. He has published three award-winning poetry chapbooks, *Bliss* (Brickhouse Books, 1998),

*Mountain Fireflies* (Poetic Matrix, 2000), and *Flint Shards from Sussex* (Gival Press, 2000); two full-length books of poetry, *Bones Washed with Wine* (Gival Press, 2003) and *On the Tongue* (Gival Press, 2006); a collection of personal essays, *Edge* (Southern Tier Editions, 2003); a novella, "Devoured," included in *Masters of Midnight: Erotic Tales of the Vampire* (Kensington, 2003); a book of poetry and memoir, *Loving Mountains, Loving Men* (Ohio University Press, 2005); and a volume of short fiction, *A History of Barbed Wire* (Suspect Thoughts Press, 2006), which won a Lambda Literary Award. He teaches creative writing at Virginia Tech in Blacksburg, Virginia.

**Blair Mastbaum** is the author of the novels *Clay's Way* (Alyson Books, 2004) and *Us Ones In Between* (Running Press, 2008), co-editor of *Cool Thing: Best New Gay Fiction* (Running Press, 2008), and judge for *Best Gay Erotica 2010*. He lives in Portland, Oregon.

**Lloyd Meeker** has published two volumes of poetry; his first novel, *The Darkness of Castle Tiralur*, was published by Torquere Press in 2007. Describing himself as a happy mystic-in-training, Meeker now lives with his husband in Vancouver, working as an energy healer, writer, and industrial camera technician.

**Elaine Miller** is a Vancouver leatherdyke with a very full life and too many projects on the go. Her writing has been anthologized in *Best Bondage Erotica 2* (Cleis Press, 2005), *Best of Best Lesbian Erotica* (Cleis Press, 2000), *Best Lesbian Erotica 2005* (Cleis Press, 2004), *Hot Lesbian Erotica 2005* (Cleis Press, 2005), *With a Rough Tongue: Femmes Write Porn* (Arsenal Pulp Press, 2006), *Best Lesbian Erotica 1998* (Cleis Press, 1999), *Best Lesbian Erotica 2001* (Cleis Press, 2000), *Exact Fare Only II* (Anvil Press, 2003), *Skin Deep 2: More Real-Life Lesbian Sex* (Alyson Books, 2004),

*Brazen Femme: Queering Femininity* (Arsenal Pulp Press, 2002), as well as various periodicals and websites. She was *Xtra! West's* monthly queer and kinky sex columnist from 2002 to 2006, and published *Diversity Magazine* (pansexual, pornographic, perverted, and political) from 1994 to 1997. Since 1993 she has been actively involved in and around the production of women's leather events. More info: *elainemiller.com*.

**Achy Obejas** is the author of the recent novel, *Ruins* (Akashic, 2009). Her two previous novels, *Days of Awe* (Ballantine, 2001), and *Memory Mambo* (Cleis, 1996), both won the Lambda Literary Award. She is also author of the short story collection *We Came All the Way from Cuba So You Could Dress Like This?* (Cleis, 1994), and the poetry collection *This Is What Happened in Our Other Life* (A Midsummer Night's Press, 2007). She edited and translated into English the anthology *Havana Noir* (Akashic, 2007) and she has translated into Spanish Junot Diaz's novel *The Brief Wondrous Life of Oscar Wao* (Riverhead Trade, 2008). An accomplished journalist, she worked at the *Chicago Tribune* for over a decade, and has also written for the *Village Voice*, the *Los Angeles Times*, *Vogue*, *Playboy*, *Ms.*, *The Nation*, *The Advocate*, *Windy City Times*, *High Performance*, *Chicago Sun-Times*, *Chicago Reader*, *Nerve.com*, *Latina*, *Out*, and others. Among her many honors, she has received a Pulitzer Prize for a *Tribune* team investigation, the Studs Terkel Journalism Prize, and several Peter Lisagor journalism honors, as well as residencies at Yaddo, Ragdale, and the Virginia Center for the Arts. She has served as Springer Writer-in-Residence at the University of Chicago and the Distinguished Writer-in-Residence at the University of Hawai'i, and is currently the Sor Juana Visiting Writer at DePaul University in Chicago.

**Joy Parks** won the Gaylactic Spectrum Award for her novelette, "Instinct," in *The Future is Queer* (Arsenal Pulp Press, 2006). She has fully recovered from her brush with lesbian celebrity, and is writing and living as normal a life as she ever expects she will, just outside of Ottawa.

**Andy Quan** has worked for gay and lesbian rights since the late 1980s, talking about sex, cultural diversity within queer communities, and more. He was the coordinator of the International Lesbian and Gay Association (ILGA) in the mid-1990s, and has since worked for the London gay men's HIV prevention agency, Rubberstuffers, and the Australian Federation of AIDS Organizations. He is the author of two books of poetry, one of short fiction, and one of gay erotica, and his writings have appeared in a broad range of anthologies and literary reviews. Born in Vancouver of Cantonese origins, he now lives in Sydney, Australia, where he works on regional and international HIV and AIDS issues. Visit him at: *andyquan.com*.

**Michael Rowe** was born in Ottawa and has lived in Beirut, Havana, Geneva, and Paris. His most recent book, *Other Men's Sons* (Cormorant Books, 2007), won the 2008 Randy Shilts Award for Nonfiction. A past winner of the Lambda Literary Award, he is also a contributing writer to *The Advocate*. He is married and lives in Toronto. He welcomes readers at *michaelrowe.com*.

**Stacia Seaman** is an editor who has worked with *New York Times* and *USA Today* bestselling authors. She has edited numerous award-winning titles, and with co-editor Radclyffe won a Lambda Literary Award for *Erotic Interludes 2: Stolen Moments* (Bold Strokes Books, 2005) and an Independent Publishers Award's silver medal and a Golden Crown Literary Award for *Erotic Interludes 4:*

*Extreme Passions* (Bold Strokes, 2005). Stacia edits everything from textbooks to popular nonfiction to mysteries and romance novels. She lives with her cat, Frieda, and enjoys being silly.

**Natty Soltesz** has had stories published in the anthologies *Best Gay Erotica 2009* (Cleis Press, 2008), *Best Gay Romance 2009* (Cleis, 2009), and *Boy Crazy* (Cleis, 2009); regularly publishes fiction in the magazines *Freshmen*, *Mandate*, and *Handjobs*; and is a faithful contributor to the Nifty Erotic Stories Archive. He's worked with director Joe Gage on a script for an upcoming porn film, and is at work on a book-length project. He lives in Pittsburgh with his boo. Check out his website: *bacteriaburger.com*.

**Jay Starre** has written for numerous gay men's magazines, including *Torso* and *Men*. His writing has also been included in over forty-five gay anthologies, including *Quickies 3* (Arsenal Pulp Press, 2003), *Best Date Ever* (Alyson Books, 2007), *Ultimate Gay Erotica 2005* and *2006* (Alyson Books), *Full Body Contact* (Alyson Books, 2002), *Travelrotica for Gay Men: Erotic Travel Adventures* (Alyson Books, 2006), and *Bears* (Cleis Press, 2008). His steamy historical novel, *The Erotic Tales of the Knights Templars* (Star Books Press), was published in 2007. He lives in Vancouver.

**Mattilda Bernstein Sycamore** is an insomniac with dreams. She is the author of two novels, *So Many Ways to Sleep Badly* (City Lights, 2008) and *Pulling Taffy* (Suspect Thoughts, 2003), and the editor of four nonfiction anthologies, most recently *Nobody Passes: Rejecting the Rules of Gender and Conformity* (Seal Press, 2007) and an expanded second edition of *That's Revolting! Queer Strategies for Resisting Assimilation* (Soft Skull Press, 2008). Mattilda is still looking for answers and loves feedback and propositions. Her homepage is *mattildabernsteinsycamore.com*.

**Jason Timermanis** is a Canadian writer and an MFA Creative Writing candidate at the University of Arizona. He is at work on his first novel.

**Jane Van Ingen** is a fundraiser who lives and works in Brooklyn. A frequent contributor to Lambda Book Report, her writing has appeared in *Eyes of Desire 2: A Deaf GLBT Reader* (Handtype Press, 2007) and Lambda Award Winner *First Person Queer* (Arsenal Pulp Press, 2007). She is also a coordinator at the Lesbian Herstory Archives in New York City.

**R.M. Vaughan** is a Toronto-based writer and video artist. His latest book is *Troubled: A Memoir in Poems and Fragments*, published by Coach House Books in 2008.

**Clarence Wong** writes fiction depicting culture collisions: gay men navigating in a straight world, Asian immigrants transplanted to a Western society. His work has appeared in anthologies, literary journals, and magazines, including *Boys in Heat* (Cleis Press, 2008), the *Harrington Gay Men's Fiction Quarterly*, and *Silver Kris*, the in-flight magazine of Singapore Airlines. A graduate of Princeton and Stanford universities, he believes in the transformative power of a good story. He lives in San Francisco.

EDITORS' BIOGRAPHIES

**Richard Labonté** has edited about two dozen erotic anthologies for Cleis Press, co-edited *The Future is Queer* and *First Person Queer* (both with Lawrence Schimel) for Arsenal Pulp Press, writes a fortnightly book review column for Q Syndicate, and transmutes turgid technical writing into bright golden prose for assorted clients. In part one of his post-university life, he wrote and edited for the *Citizen* newspaper in Ottawa, Ontario; in part two, he helped found and eventually managed A Different Light Bookstores in Los Angeles, West Hollywood, San Francisco, and New York; in part three— since returning to Canada in 2001—he has been self-employed as a freelance editor and reviewer. He lives on Bowen Island, British Columbia, with his partner, Asa Liles.

**Lawrence Schimel** is a full-time author and anthologist who has published more than ninety books, including *The Future is Queer* (with Richard Labonté; Arsenal Pulp), *Best Gay Poetry* 2008 (A Midsummer Night's Press / Lethe Press), *Best Date Ever: True Stories That Celebrate Gay Relationships* (Alyson), *Two Boys in Love* (Seventh Window), *The Drag Queen of Elfland* (Circlet), *The Mammoth Book of New Gay Erotica* (Carroll & Graf), and *Fairy Tales for Writers* (A Midsummer Night's Press), among others. Writing in Spanish, his books include the poetry collection *Desayuno en la cama* (Desatada / Egales), the graphic novel *Vacaciones en Ibiza* (Egales), and the children's books *Amigos y vecinos* (Ediciones La Librería), *La aventura de Cecilia y el dragón* (Bibliópolis), and *Cosas que puedo hacer yo solo* (Macmillan), among others. *First Person Queer* (with Richard Labonté; Arsenal Pulp) won a Lambda Literary Award in 2008, and his *PoMoSexuals: Challenging Assumptions About Gender and Sexuality* (with Carol Queen; Cleis) won a Lambda Literary Award in 1998; he has also been a finalist for the Lambda Literary Award eleven other times. The German edition of his anthology *Switch Hitters: Lesbians Write Gay Male Erotica and Gay Men Write Lesbian Erotica* (with Carol Queen; Cleis) won the Siegesseuele Best Book of the Year Award. He won the Rhysling Award for Poetry in 2002. His children's book *No hay nada como el original* (Destino) was selected by the International Youth Library in Munich for the White Ravens 2005, and his children's book *¿Lees un libro conmigo?* (Destino) was selected by the International Board of Books for Young People as an Outstanding Books for Young People with Disabilities 2007. His work has been widely anthologized in *The Random House Book of Science Fiction Stories*, *The Best of Best Gay Erotica*, *Gay Love Poetry*, *The Sandman: The Book of Dreams*, *Chicken Soup for the Horse-Lover's Soul 2*, and *The Random House Treasury of Light Verse*, among many others. He has also contributed to numerous periodicals, from *The Christian Science Monitor* to *Physics Today* to *Gay Times*. His writings have been translated into Basque, Catalan, Croatian, Czech, Dutch, Esperanto, Finnish, French, Galician, German, Greek, Hungarian, Icelandic, Indonesian, Italian, Japanese, Polish, Portuguese, Romanian, Russian, Serbian, Slovene, Slovak, and Spanish. For two years he served as co-chair of the Publishing Triangle, a US organization of lesbians and gay men in the publishing industry, and he also served as the Regional Advisor of the Spain Chapter of the Society of Children's Book Writers and Illustrators for five years. Born in New York City in 1971, he lives in Madrid, Spain.